REMEMBERING

Rutherford

REMEMBERING

Rutherford

GREG TUCKER

Charleston   London

THE
History
PRESS

Published by The History Press
Charleston, SC 29403
www.historypress.net

Copyright © 2010 by Greg Tucker
All rights reserved

First published 2010

Manufactured in the United States

ISBN 978.1.59629.949.8

Library of Congress Cataloging-in-Publication Data

Tucker, Greg
Remembering Rutherford / Greg Tucker.
p. cm.
Includes bibliographical references.
ISBN 978-1-59629-949-8
1. Rutherford County (Tenn.)--History--Anecdotes. 2. Rutherford County (Tenn.)--History,
Local--Anecdotes. 3. Rutherford County (Tenn.)--Social life and customs--Anecdotes. 4.
Rutherford County (Tenn.)--Biography--Anecdotes. I. Title.
F443.R8T83 2010
976.8'57--dc22
2010006752

Contents

CONTENTS

Dedication and Acknowledgement

This first volume of anecdotal history is dedicated to my most avid reader and honest critic—my wife and partner, Minh-Triet. I am also indebted to the *Daily News Journal*, our hometown newspaper, and its senior management—Andrew Oppmann, Jimmy Hart, Gary Frazier, Sam Stockard and Jim Davis. My sincerest thanks go to the many *Remembering Rutherford* readers who have provided information and encouragement. All proceeds from the sale of this volume benefit the Children's Discovery Center at Murfree Spring, Murfreesboro, Tennessee.

I

EARLY SETTLEMENT AND
THE CIVIL WAR

EARLY WATER SOURCE, SAND SPRING,
NOW A CITY DRAIN

Sand Spring, once a place of natural beauty and later an urban "mud hole,"
is now part of a protected wetland and an educational resource. Where
water was once drawn, water is now discharged.

When the Tennessee General Assembly appointed seven town
commissioners in October 1811 "to fix on a place" for the county seat in
Rutherford County, the legislators specified that the location should be "as
near the center of said County as a suitable situation can be procured,
having due respect to good water." A year later, when the commissioners
settled on the site offered by Captain William Lytle—sixty acres of his
own land—the abundance of streams and springs was duly noted, and
Murfreesboro was located.

With respect to "good water" for this new town, Sand Spring was particularly
impressive, located no more than nine hundred yards south of the courthouse.
Sixty years later, in 1870, John C. Spence documented the character of this
source, based on firsthand recollections of early town inhabitants:

> *Sand Spring* [when the town was first settled] *was one of the finest in
> the country, having a large broad basin, moderately deep, clear water. In the
> center, through a hole in a rock, white sand came boiling up with the water*

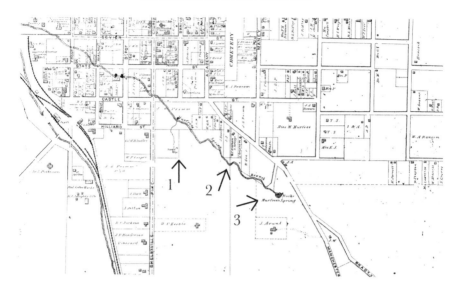

This 1908 map of the southwest corner of Murfreesboro shows Sand Springs (1), Murfree Spring Branch (aka Town Creek) (2) and Murfree Spring (3). *Map from the Rutherford County Archives.*

---

in a bold manner, which gave the name "Sand Springs." This was a never failing spring, the water cool and refreshing at all times. The water passing off in a bold manner through the undergrowth to the neighboring stream, the Murfree Spring branch.

City dwellers used the spring and its surroundings for leisure, as well as a water source, hauling the water in horse-drawn "water drays and negros in pots on the head."

The Spence description, supplemented by deed descriptions, places the Sand Spring about 350 feet east of South Church Street, behind the current R.J. Young office. The confluence of the Sand Spring and Murfree Spring branches would have been about 100 feet east of South Church, behind what is now the KFC site.

The Spence description continues:

The surrounding large overcup acorn trees, red oak, sweet gum and other trees, these all thickly standing over the ground, casting a deep shade over the spring during the day, keeping the water at a cool temperature. Near by the spring, large moss covered rocks, lying piled intermixed with heavy growing timber…Just at the base, a large long projecting rock [with] two…caves

angling back some sixty feet, where they join, three by four feet, running
along the solid rock, same size, all the way without a break in the walls…
Little boys visiting the Sand Spring were sure to make a visit to these caves.

But by 1825, the town aldermen were considering the need to "have
the Sand Spring put in good order," and in the 1830s a scheme to pipe
water directly from Sand Spring to the center of town failed. By the time
Spence wrote his history in 1870, earlier efforts to enlarge the spring had
destroyed and removed all of the rocks, timber and caves. Much of the rock
was blasted and hauled away for foundations and roadway in the growing
community. "Time and improvement have swept them all away, blasted,
gone," concluded Spence. "Still affording a good supply of water, but not so
cooling as in time past."

Soon after the Civil War, the "Sand Spring lot" was acquired by Camillus
B. Huggins, a land dealer and speculator who bought and sold literally
hundreds of land parcels in and around the growing county seat during
the last half of the nineteenth century. Huggins leased the spring and
surrounding property to the Nashville, Chattanooga & St. Louis Railroad
(NC&St.L) as a water supply for the steam-driven locomotives. During this
occupancy, the Sand Spring branch was filled in, and a rock-lined basin was
built to hold a supply of water for use by the railroad. Overflow water spread
across the lot and formed the mud hole.

The railroad lease ended with Huggins's death, and in 1910 his widow
sold the Sand Spring lot to yet another land speculator and businessman,
E.B. James, whose holdings included a very successful stable and carriage
house on the west side of South Church filling the block between West
Castle and Hilliard Streets, as many as one hundred tenant houses spread
across the southern third of the town and several turnpike projects. Except
for the portion of the property fronting on South Church, the mud hole
remained idle and undeveloped for the next fifty years, as title passed down
through the James family. In time, trees and undergrowth filled in the area
around the mud hole, and the emerging marsh joined with the widening
marsh below Murfree Spring, the icehouse and the city waterworks. Higher
ground around the spring provided pasture for James' livestock.

In 1946, the local radio station (WGNS) leased part of the pasture for
placement of a radio broadcast tower. The tower became a permanent
fixture in 2001, when Guy James Jr. sold the tower plot to station owner Bart
Walker. (The tower remains today as the only privately owned property in
the midst of what is now officially designated as protected wetlands.) Since

1950, several city drainage projects have diverted runoff from residential areas onto the Sand Spring lot, reversing the early water consumption activity and soaking even the higher ground.

The Sand Spring lot and adjacent properties were acquired by a state agency in 2000 and transferred to the City of Murfreesboro in connection with the development of the Discovery Center. The protected wetlands environment is now under the U.S. Army Corps of Engineers' jurisdiction and is jointly maintained by the Murfreesboro Parks and Recreation Department, the Army Corps of Engineers and the Discovery Center. Although vastly different from its original state, the Sand Spring's legacy is today a valued and enjoyed ecological learning center with an expanding wildlife population.

TOWN CREEK ONCE NAVIGATED FOR "BRAGGING RIGHTS"

Local hatter and hides dealer Alfred Miller was a shrewd businessman and adventurer, but some of his contemporaries in early nineteenth-century Murfreesboro politely called him "eccentric."

Soon after the establishment of Murfreesboro, Miller decided to make a trip to New Orleans to purchase inventory for his business, but also for adventure and "bragging rights." His plan was to make the entire trip by water from Murfree Spring to New Orleans. To this end, he built himself a light wood skiff, launched it at the mouth of the spring and poled down the branch without obstruction. He then worked his way down Lytle Creek to the Stones River and continued rowing, stopping to carry his boat and gear around several milldams and shoals, until he reached the Cumberland River and eventually Nashville.

Selling his skiff in Nashville for one dollar, he secured passage on a keelboat and floated down the Cumberland, Ohio and Mississippi Rivers to his destination. "Had a mighty good time" on the downriver trip, he reported whenever he had occasion to brag of being the only person to navigate the trip from the Murfree Spring. The upstream return trip, however, loaded with merchandise from some sharp trading, was rather arduous. The roundtrip required three months, with the return voyage consuming eight to ten weeks.

A similar navigation today would be frustrated from the start by shallow marshes, scenic walkways, culverts, pipes and numerous hazards, but modern day's relatively inconspicuous Murfree Spring Creek was for many generations a prominent part of the city landscape.

In the beginning, quite literally, the creek was significant in the layout of the original town lots. When Hugh Robinson, a town commissioner and surveyor, first laid out the town lots in 1812, he used the mouth of Murfree Spring Branch on Lytle Creek as the zero point on the survey. (The branch is frequently called Town Creek in local writings and on some maps. On at least one engineering plat from the 1940s, the branch has the name Harrells Creek.)

As in many cities in the late nineteenth and early twentieth centuries, a flowing stream served as a waste disposal channel, and Murfreesboro was no exception. This convenience of the creek surely influenced the location of several local enterprises during post–Civil War industrialization.

Flowing in an open channel in 1910, the creek crossed the intersection of Castle and South Church Streets (about fifty yards south of the current Broad and Church intersection). There was a wooden bridge for Castle and a stone bridge for Church.

Flowing diagonally through the city block between South Church and South Maple, the creek crossed South Maple under a wooden bridge about three blocks south of the courthouse, where the Copymatte Printing Co. is today. Just south of the creek, on the corner of South Maple and West Castle, was the steam laundry. On Castle behind the laundry backing against the creek was the electric generating plant owned by the Murfreesboro Gas & Light Co. Directly across the creek facing on West State was the W.T. James Wool Carding plant.

The creek continued diagonally across the West State and South Walnut intersection, under another wooden bridge just north of the Elliott Cotton Gin. Flowing northwest through the city block between South Walnut and South Front Streets (now the Shoney's and Longhorn Liquors property between Broad and Hickerson), the creek was accessible behind the seed warehouse on South Walnut and the Rather & Maney Cotton Gin. Crossing South Front just south of the intersection with West Sevier, the creek went under another wooden bridge and flowed through the middle of the Williams Bros. Lumberyard (now the green space around the Cannonsburgh office building).

Flowing north under one of the large lumber sheds, the creek left the lumberyard and crossed West Sevier under another wooden bridge. Turning west, the creek passed the Ransom Grain Warehouse and flowed along the Ransom Stockyard before reaching its mouth on Lytle Creek under the railroad bridge. (The Ransom businesses filled the area that is now the Cannonsburgh/Greenway parking lot and green space behind several businesses on Broad.)

Efforts to clean up the creek began with Depression-era projects in the 1930s, but the most dramatic changes began in 1949, when city engineers developed plans for the new Broad Street and drainage of the flood-plagued southwest sector of the downtown area. According to plan, Town Creek mostly disappeared under pavement, following a route south of the Broad Street right of way and serving as a primary storm drain for much of the city.

Today, the creek flows from the Discovery Center wetlands into a large culvert behind KFC on the east side of South Church, angles under Church to the southwest corner of the Broad and Church intersection and then flows under the sidewalk past the Subway shop, making a sharp turn south to Hickerson Drive, where it again heads west under Hickerson. (This stretch was rechanneled to divert the creek from the original streambed that looped north of Broad Street. A substantial portion of the city's storm water drainage passes through this section of the buried creek.) From Hickerson, the creek angles northwest and reemerges in a channelized streambed that flows alongside Cannonsburgh to the original mouth on Lytle Creek.

Once a "navigable" water source, later a waste stream and now an important part of the city's storm drain system, Murfree Spring Branch, aka Town Creek, aka Harrells Creek, continues to play a significant role in the city's infrastructure.

Private Investors Fueled County Infrastructure Growth

The local smart money was investing in Rutherford County infrastructure in the mid-1800s, replacing the trails, footpaths and wagon roads with "modern turnpikes."

In 1816, John L. McAdam, a Scotsman, developed a process for road surfacing using crushed stone bound with gravel (later coal tar) on a bed of larger stones, with the center of the road higher than the edges. McAdam's process for producing hard, durable road surfaces—known as macadam or tarmac—was first used in the United States in 1830 and prompted a boom in road building.

In 1831, the Tennessee legislature began development of the first "turnpike" through Rutherford County by appointing an Internal Improvement Board empowered to solicit stock subscriptions for "a turnpike road from Nashville to Murfreesboro and Shelbyville." The Rutherford appointees were Henry D. Jamison, Samuel Anderson and Vernon D. Cowens.

The legislature specified that when $50,000 had been subscribed, the governor could add $60,000 from the "common school fund." The stock solicitation could then continue until a total of $260,000 was available for the project. The fundraising was to be completed within six months. This early enactment gave no specifications for construction or operation of the road—one of the first in the state.

The first ten-mile segment of the project, between Nashville and Murfreesboro, was contracted to John and James Holmes, "two energetic and somewhat eccentric Irishmen." The initial groundbreaking on July 4, 1832, was a festive event with much oratory and toasting. The road was completed by 1842, but soon there were issues regarding quality of construction, maintenance, operation and tolls.

In 1850, typically playing catch-up, the legislature adopted standards and procedures for turnpike development. The statute contemplated the exclusive use of private funding with the state giving free access over state property. The power of condemnation was also given to the private turnpike companies once a route was approved.

The state specified that turnpikes must be planked or macadamized and bedded at least twenty-four feet wide. Even the depth and size of gravel was specified. Whether bridges were to be built, as opposed to fording or ferrying, was left to the discretion of county authorities. The companies were even given the power to take needed material (timber, gravel, dirt) from private land with condemnation powers if the landowner disputed the company's offer of "fair compensation."

Tollgates were permitted every five miles, and tolls could be levied as follows:

One cent per head for hogs or sheep, two cents per head for cattle or horses or mules in a drove; for horses or mules not in a drove nor employed in drawing, five cents per head, whether mounted or not; for every loaded wagon twenty-five cents; for buggies and barouches and other similar two-horse carriages fifteen cents; other two-horse pleasure carriages twenty-five cents; for one-horse buggies and other similar vehicles for the conveyance of persons, 10 cents; other vehicles for the transportation of goods or produce, 10 cents.

New turnpikes could not begin collecting tolls until a panel of "disinterested" inspectors confirmed construction quality. Maintenance could be forced by any citizen or road user by complaint to any local justice or magistrate. Toll collection could be suspended until needed maintenance was completed. Stiff fines were also set for failure to pay tolls and for damaging gates or roadways.

With the rules clearly defined, the turnpike investment pace accelerated. Prominent Rutherford names began to appear and repeat on company charters. The Murfreesboro to Woodbury Turnpike Company was incorporated in 1851 by Charles Ready and William Spence (Murfreesboro); John Hall and Enoch Jones (Halls Hill); John Peay (Readyville); and R.H. Mason (Woodbury). This road project was allowed to substitute river gravel for crushed stone.

The Murfreesboro to Franklin Company included familiar names like Spence, Maney, Lytle and Critchlow. The Murfreesboro to Liberty (through Halls Hill) Turnpike Company was incorporated by Spence, Jones and Dennis Hogwood. They agreed to use Jacob Wright's bridge over the Stones River East Fork.

Turnpike ownership and construction affected the county boundary to the southwest. Eagleville was a thriving Williamson County community that wanted a modern, direct road link to the county seat in Franklin. When no investors showed interest in a western road, Rutherford investors (Richard and James A. Ransom) agreed, in 1877, to build a turnpike linking Eagleville with the new Murfreesboro to Salem turnpike. Seeing their future more closely tied to Murfreesboro, Eagleville leaders successfully petitioned the legislature for inclusion in Rutherford County. (If you were on your way to church on the Eagleville to Salem road, no tolls were charged.)

Spence, L.H. Carney, Levi Reeves, E.A. Keeble, Dr. S.H. Woods and others incorporated the Bradyville Turnpike Company in 1852. Some fifty years later, Elmo Burr James was sole owner of this thoroughfare. Guy James Jr. remembers stories of his grandfather riding the pike in horse and buggy periodically to collect funds from the tollgate keepers and to inspect for repairs and maintenance. "He would set out from Murfreesboro in the morning with a supply of good whiskey, spend the night with a friend in Bradyville, resupply and ride back on the following day." James would then send out his son and a black laborer named Steve Mix to do the repairs.

In 1856, the Hoover's Gap to Christiana and the Murfreesboro to Middleton Turnpike Companies were established. Henry Hoover of Hoover's

Gap and John Miller in Christiana organized their venture. The Middleton project was yet another venture led by William Spence. (Middleton was later renamed Midland to accommodate the post office.) *Goodspeed's History of Rutherford County* (1886) observed: "It is doubtful that any county in the State can boast as many and as good pikes."

The late Clifton Stephens, one of the last tollgate keepers, remembered the Cainsville turnpike, which began at the junction and terminus of the Jefferson and Murfreesboro to Lascassas turnpikes. The gate was a long pole hinged to the porch corner of the family home. When closed, the gate hooked to a large cedar tree.

Stephens remembered that a pony cart carrying two children to school passed for five cents. The local hearse pulled by two horses had to pay a quarter, but funeral processions were not charged. The late fall turkey drives were supposed to pay a penny per bird, but usually they just left a couple of birds for the toll. At night, the gate was left open so travelers would not disturb the sleeping Stephens family.

Although quite profitable for several decades, by the end of the nineteenth century few of the Rutherford roads were operating much above break-even. As turnpikes were neglected or abandoned, the state attached the company assets, and the roads became the responsibility of the state or county. The last turnpike toll in Rutherford County was probably paid by someone driving a Ford Model T.

PEAS AND SWEET POTATOES MARKED SURRENDER ANNIVERSARY

Recently, a local group of historians and like-minded friends gathered for an anniversary, which they observed by dining on black-eyed peas, sweet potatoes and birthday cake at Oaklands. They billed the occasion as "Ole Bedford's Black Eye Pea and Sweet Potato Supper."

The occasion was the 146th anniversary of the June 13, 1862 raid on Murfreesboro led by Nathan Bedford Forrest. Anyone with even a passing interest in local Civil War history knows that Forrest and his mounted troops surprised the occupying Union forces with an attack focusing on the Rutherford County Courthouse, where the Federals had imprisoned most of the leading citizens of Cannon County, as well as a number of

Oaklands—where victor and vanquished shared a meager meal. *Original sketch by David "Wegee" Weigant; charcoal rendering by Minh-Triet Tucker. (Weigant, a prominant Rutherford County illustrator, succumbed to cancer before finishing this project. Tucker, a friend and admirer of his work, completed this rendering of the dinner table surrender of Murfreesboro. A special thanks to Sharon Petty, Carriage Lane Inn, Murfreesboro, and to the reenactors of Murfreesboro, Camp #33, Sons of Confederate Veterans.)*

prominent local citizens. The prisoners were facing possible execution as secessionist traitors.

Although Forrest is one of the more controversial personalities of the Civil War era, it is quite likely that a significant number of descendants of the "old families" of this area—particularly in Cannon County and Woodbury—would not be here today if Forrest and his men had not succeeded in freeing the courthouse prisoners.

The early morning raid caught the Union forces unprepared for battle. The fighting resulted in 229 casualties. Forrest lost 30 men, with 60 wounded, compared to 19 Union deaths and 120 wounded. By making the Federal commanders believe they were outnumbered, the raiders gained an unconditional surrender. The Confederates captured about 1,200 Federal soldiers, half a million dollars' worth of munitions and supplies, sixty wagons, 175 horses, 300 mules and four cannons. The surrender papers were signed by Union General T.T. Crittenden at Oaklands.

But why black-eyed peas and sweet potatoes? According to oral histories maintained by the Oaklands Museum, after the surrender was signed at the dining room table in the Maney home, the Maney family served a meal for Forrest and the surrendering officers. Some years later, Rachel Maney explained that it was not an impressive table: "The Yankees had killed every peafowl, every duck, every cow on the place. That night we ate baked sweet potatoes and black-eyed peas."

The idea for an anniversary dinner of black-eyed peas and sweet potatoes was suggested by James Patterson, adjutant for the Sons of Confederate Veterans Camp #33. The first anniversary meal was held at Oaklands in July 1999. Patterson, an avid Civil War reenactor, explains that the supper is now established as an annual observance.

And the birthday cake? Coincidentally, the Murfreesboro raid took place on Forrest's forty-first birthday. His birth date—July 13, 1821—is memorialized in Tennessee Codes Annotated, section 15-2-101, which authorizes the governor to proclaim July 13 as Nathan Bedford Forrest Day.

So who is "Ole Bedford"? At least two Civil War historians/authors, Robert S. Henry and John A. Wyeth, confirm that some of those who rode with Nathan Bedford Forrest called him, respectfully, "Old Bedford"—perhaps recognizing that he was twice the age of many of those young men under his command.

A special thank-you to Nila Gober, Oaklands Museum, for research assistance.

THE COURTHOUSE SYCAMORE

The tree that stands at the southeast corner of the courthouse, across from the old Goldstein's Department Store building (now county offices), is bound to be the largest sycamore in Rutherford County. The circumference at four feet up the trunk is sixteen and a half feet.

Sycamores, as we all know, generally grow along riverbanks and creeks or in marshy areas. They require a lot of water. So how has this giant prospered high and dry amidst concrete and asphalt? It has to have found a stream or reservoir

The Miller brothers—Brad, Billy and Ebby—with the 160-year-old sycamore planted on the square by several of their ancestors before the Civil War. *Courtesy of the* Daily News Journal, *Murfreesboro.*

of water under the square and gotten its roots well down in this natural flow. Since we know that there was at least one hand-dug well on the square, it is reasonable to expect that water is still there—and the growth of this tree so indicates.

JUDGE ROYCE TAYLOR was adding trees to his yard a few years ago and decided that something rooted in local history would be appropriate. He picked up a sycamore seedpod from the courthouse lawn, shook out a number of seeds and planted several in a pot. Now he has two descendants of the historic, 160-year-old courthouse sycamore in his yard, one of which has reached a height of about twelve feet.

The sycamore, or plane tree, is a native North American species. The hard, yellowish to brown, close-grained wood has limited uses, and very few sycamores are commercially harvested. The round seedpods are nearly as big as ping-pong balls and can be a nuisance underfoot, especially on pavement. The pods are called "buttons," and some folks refer to the tree as buttonwood. Others regard it as a "weed tree."

According to C.C. Henderson in *The Story of Murfreesboro* (1929), the courthouse tree was planted about 1850 by Alfred, Isaac and Austin Miller. They originally planted four trees, one at each corner, but only this one has survived. Brad Miller, a descendant of the early Millers, says that the trees came from along the Stones River on the family plantation about three and a half miles due south of the square. According to Miller family lore, Alfred and Austin fished while field hands dug, wrapped and loaded the trees for mules to haul to the square, where they were planted consistent with the wishes of the county court. Whether the Millers donated the labor or trees or the family received payment from the county is long since forgotten.

County deed records show that in 1815 Robert, Matthew, Isaac, William and John Miller assembled a five-hundred-acre farm along the West Fork of Stones River at the mouths of the Long, Henry and Crooked Creeks. But these were the "Christiana Millers," unrelated to Alfred and Austin, says Brad Miller. Alfred was a successful Murfreesboro hatter who also traded in notes receivable. In the 1840s, Alfred purchased two thousand acres south of town for eight dollars per acre. The Miller family cemetery on the west side of South Church (Shelbyville Highway) today evidences the location of the once prosperous estate. Alfred later served as mayor of Murfreesboro during the Civil War occupation.

Henderson's 1929 history reports that at one time poplar trees were planted on three sides of the courthouse, perhaps replacing the sycamores that didn't survive, but these were also gone by the 1920s. According to Henderson, John Nelson, "an early surveyor," planted the poplars.

TWO PILOT KNOBS

Delmer Lowe insists that a particular southeast Rutherford County hill near the Big Springs community is Pilot Knob. He should know the territory since his kinfolk have collectively owned the hill and surrounding property for several generations.

But an exhibit at the Heritage Center, 225 West College Street in Murfreesboro, entitled Place Names of Rutherford County stated: "Pilot Knob, located along the Woodbury Highway near Readyville, is the highest hill in the county with its peak reaching over eleven hundred feet high."

Actually, the Pilot Knob near Readyville is 1,233 feet high, but it is not the highest hill in the county. It is not even the highest Pilot Knob in Rutherford County. According to Tennessee Valley Authority (TVA) and U.S. Geologic Survey maps, the highest Pilot Knob in Rutherford County is due south of the Big Springs community in the southeast section of the county. That's Delmer's hill. Officially named "Pilot Knob" and marked as 1,305 feet above sea level, the Big Springs Pilot Knob stands above the Readyville knob of the same name by 72 feet.

Why do two hills in Rutherford County bear the same name? The term "pilot" in its most generic sense, according to Webster's dictionary, means "to guide or lead in a straight and/or safe way." Early American explorers and travelers were guided by landmarks, and any hill that stood out as unique or distinct was likely to be relied on as a "pilot." A "knob" is defined by Webster's as "an isolated prominent rounded hill." Both Pilot Knobs in Rutherford County satisfy this description. The Readyville knob could certainly have been a guiding landmark, or pilot, for travelers heading east from Black Fox Springs, and the Big Springs knob could have been a significant pilot for those on the old "war trail" heading for what is now known as Hoover's Gap. "Pilot Knob" is a common descriptive name most likely dating from the period of early exploration and settlement.

Official records of the Civil War confirm that Union forces used the Pilot Knob near Readyville for "signal communications with Murfreesborough," as evidenced in communication from Union major general T.L. Crittenden to his superior on June 24, 1863, from Donald's Church on Bradyville Pike. Local Civil War historian Wayne Reed recalls that remnants of stone and earthen fortifications could still be identified on the knob until a few years ago when they were bulldozed flat by a

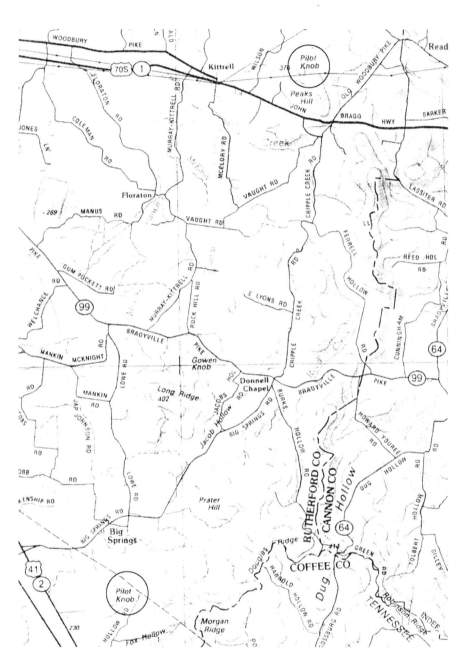

Map of southeast Rutherford County showing two Pilot Knobs. *Map reproduced from U.S. Geological Survey publications (revised 1974 and 1980).*

former property owner. Based on interpretation of official Union records, Reed suggests that "Fort Transit" was how Union forces identified their Pilot Knob base.

A more significant Pilot Knob in Tennessee Civil War history is near the Tennessee River and is the highest point in West Tennessee, according to Civil War historian Randy Bishop. This site is now part of the Nathan Bedford Forrest State Park and overlooks Johnsonville Landing, where Forrest's cavalry destroyed thirty-five Union vessels and captured about ninety-five thousand tons of quartermaster supplies.

A quick map check found over one hundred "Pilot Knobs" in the United States. The highest Pilot Knob in Tennessee is about sixteen hundred feet in Greene County in East Tennessee.

Where is the highest hill in Rutherford County? Several notable contenders are: Ruckers Knob, where Rutherford, Wilson and Cannon Counties originally cornered at 1,315 feet; Long Ridge, where Cripple Creek rises at 1,320 feet; and the Tennessee Valley Divide west of Hoover's Gap, which divides the Cumberland River and Tennessee River watersheds, at 1,340 feet. The highest point, according to the Division of Geology, Tennessee Department of Environment and Conservation (unpublished Bulletin 86 coauthored by Ralph O. Fullerton of Murfreesboro), is 1,365 feet above sea level on Webb Ridge just north of the tri-corner junction of Rutherford, Coffee and Cannon Counties.

CELLAR EXCAVATION LED TO CEMETERY DILEMMA

Headstone number 6135 in the United States National Cemetery at the site of the Civil War Stones River Battlefield reads: "This grave contains the remains of eleven unknown soldiers." Three spaces away, headstone number 6138 states: "Three Unknown U.S. Soldiers." Is the omission of "U.S." on the first headstone significant or merely coincidental?

In February 1880, Thomas Frame, superintendent of the Stones River National Cemetery, wrote to his superior in Louisville reporting that soldier remains had been discovered on a nearby farm. T.H. Allen, a tenant on the Burrus farm about a mile west of the U.S. cemetery on what is now Asbury Road, was digging a cellar under his log house when he found human bones in a shallow grave. Mixed with the bones were brass buttons with an eagle emblem and scraps of blue cloth. Allen and Dr. Burrus believed that there were as many as three Union soldier remains under the house and were willing to have the floor taken up so the remains could be removed.

One month later, the quartermaster general of the U.S. Army ordered that "the remains of Union Soldiers…be disinterred and placed in the [Stones River] National Cemetery."

Work began immediately on the Burrus farm. (The name of the farm owner is given several different spellings. "Burrus" appears most likely to be correct based on land and genealogy records. Cemetery records also refer to Burrus as "the Doctor." Other records indicate that a Dr. William L. Burrus, grandson of Charles Ready, a Rutherford County founder, was practicing in Rutherford County in the 1870s.)

Headstone number 6135 in the National Cemetery at the Stones River National Battlefield. *Courtesy of the* Daily News Journal, *Murfreesboro.*

Circumstances changed, however, during excavation. On March 22, 1880, the officer in charge of the excavation reported:

> *After the floor of the cabin was taken up and I had dug into what seemed a grave, I found instead a pit or trench out of which I took up the remains of Eleven Soldiers. They were buried with their heads East and West placed close together. The trench was 9 feet long by about 6 feet wide. Some of them was buried North and South on the top of lower tier apparently two deep. Their bones could not be separated.*

But the greater quantity of remains was not the primary concern. The report continues:

I cannot Certify that they are Union Soldiers…I found many Union Military buttons in the trench. Also, Confederate buttons in Equal number…Union and Confederate Soldiers [were] buried in the trench together. I have all the bones…in a large box. What will I do with them?

The National Cemetery was established soon after the Civil War as a final resting place and memorial for those who had died defending the Union. The task of gathering and burying the Confederate dead was left to the local populace. Most of the Confederate dead were buried at or near where they fell. In 1867, the known Confederate remains were gathered and moved to the original Confederate cemetery two miles south of Murfreesboro on the Shelbyville Highway. In 1891, the Ladies' Memorial Association had the remains removed to the Confederate Circle, a mass grave at Evergreen Cemetery in Murfreesboro. Within the ten thousand square feet of the circle are the remains of nearly two thousand Confederate soldiers, mostly unknown.

On April 12, 1880, the National Cemetery superintendent in Murfreesboro, Tennessee, was advised that, by order of the quartermaster general of the U.S. Army, the disinterred remains of eleven unknown soldiers "be all placed in one grave at the cemetery under your charge" with a "suitable headstone." On May 6, 1880, U.S. cemetery superintendent Thomas Frame confirmed placement of headstone number 6135.

So how many Confederate soldiers killed in fighting near the Stones River are known to have been buried in the U.S. National Cemetery? At least five, maybe six.

This column was based, in part, on little-known documents from over a century ago. Grammar and capitalization within quoted portions have been kept true to the original writings.

YANKEE ENGRAVERS LEFT NAMES ON STONES RIVER ROCK

Two professionally engraved names adorn a sheer stone bluff above Stones River near the country club golf course. Marked with flourishes and dated May 20, 1864, the engravings name Daniel C. Miller and J.C. Bauhof and further identify "Co. B 115 O.V.I." The existence of the curious engravings has been known to generations of local residents.

Jim Haynes remembers when he was a child and his grandmother told him about the engraved names on the river bluff across from the family farm. But on the eve of the Civil War centennial, the circumstances surrounding the engravings were still a local mystery. The Union military connection was obvious from the date and the identification of the 115th Ohio Volunteer Infantry, but how the professional quality of the inscriptions was accomplished and what role the named individuals played were only matters of speculation.

In May 1961, Homer Pittard, a local college professor and historian, announced that he had "found" the name "Daniel C. Miller" and the identification of the Ohio military unit on a rock near the Stones River. He also reported that through official U.S. military and Ohio cemetery records he had identified and contacted Miller's descendants and had been given access to Civil War artifacts and correspondence carefully preserved and retained by the family. The correspondence consisted of forty letters written by Miller to his family while based in and around Rutherford County.

What is particularly curious about Pittard's "find" and subsequent writings on the subject is his apparent failure to see the second name and

The name "Daniel C. Miller" was engraved on a bluff over the Stones River by one of the Union soldiers and Ohio monument makers responsible for engraving the first monument on the Stones River Battlefield. *Photograph by Kevin G. Tucker.*

date on the bluff. The "J.C. Bauhof" inscription and date (May 20, 1864) are approximately two feet higher on the rock face and about three feet to the right as the bluff curves away from the river. Standing directly in front of the Miller inscription, the Bauhof name, which is more faded from exposure to the elements, could be overlooked.

Bauhof and Miller were German immigrants and professional stonecutters before enlisting with the Ohio volunteers. According to the correspondence and information Pittard obtained from the descendants, Miller and Bauhof were related, and Miller had probably been employed before the war by Bauhof, who owned "a monument works in Ohio, prior to joining the Ohio regiment."

The Ohio unit was organized and trained for guard duty at military prisons and supply depots. It was detailed to Fort Rosencrans in late 1863 to protect the critically important railroad line and the Union stores at the fort near Murfreesboro. As revealed in the correspondence, it was an easy detail by military standards of that time, and many in the unit were assigned other duties building stockades and repairing the railroad bed.

In early 1864, Bauhof and Miller were assigned and equipped to engrave the stone monument that had been erected in 1863 to commemorate the valor and success of Hazen's brigade during the Battle of Stones River. The brigade had occupied some of the most contested ground astride the railroad. Hazen's men were the only Union soldiers to hold their position throughout the fighting on December 31, 1862. They repelled four attacks that day and, on January 2, helped push back the final Confederate attack. The brigade suffered 409 casualties, including 45 who died in battle. Survivors of the battle built the monument (which is said to be the first memorial built to honor Civil War dead) during the spring of 1863.

In contrast to the experience of Hazen's brigade, Miller wrote in 1864 that he and his peers were living "like Cincinnati gentlemen." They netted fish daily, hired two ex-slaves as cooks and enjoyed a variety of fruits and meat from surrounding farms. Miller was also something of an entrepreneur, making and selling engraved silver jewelry, picture frames, tobacco boxes, axe handles and carved canes to his fellow soldiers. On the day after the date on the riverside inscriptions, Miller wrote that he and "Christie" (as Miller referred to Bauhof in his letters) occasionally took long walks through the surrounding countryside to ease the monotony of their work. When Miller was detailed to other duties, Bauhof apparently stayed on the monument assignment and completed the work.

Pittard, who served as the official Rutherford County historian from 1965 until his death in 1981, reported in 1961 that copies of the forty Miller letters were being placed in the Middle Tennessee State College library collection. The letters were written in German and were eventually translated by Mrs. Phil Howard and Ortrum Gilbert. In 1986, Mabel Pittard, widow of the county historian, published thirty of the translated letters with her own commentary. But like the report in 1961, her writing includes no mention of the Bauhof inscription and incorrectly relegates the senior artisan to only a supporting role.

DID A YANKEE SYMPATHIZER PROMOTE SAM DAVIS LEGEND?

With the cooperation of the occupying Union army leadership, John C. Kennedy retrieved the body of Sam Davis in December 1863. He also brought home a tale of courage and loyalty that established the young Confederate spy as the "boy hero of the Confederacy."

"I will die a thousand deaths before I will betray a friend" were the famous words attributed to Sam Davis, hanged as a spy for refusing to betray a friend to save his own life. The Sam Davis home, a memorial to Smyrna's most significant individual in Civil War history, attracts fourteen thousand visitors annually.

Several mysteries color the Davis legend. Historians generally agree, as did many of his contemporaries, that Davis was betrayed and identified to his Yankee captors by one of his contacts. Who exposed him, and did Davis know before his death the identity of his betrayer? Also, who was Kennedy, and what connection did he have with the occupying army and the Davis family?

Before his capture, Davis was part of the Coleman Scouts, who were scouting and spying on the Union army in Middle Tennessee. Operating under the authority of General Braxton Bragg and commanded by "E. Coleman," aka Captain Shaw, the spy network included several civilians, soldiers and at least two women—Mary Kate Patterson and Robbie Woodruff. (At least one source notes that Davis and Woodruff "were an item" with "thoughts of marriage.")

Ironically, the friend Davis refused to identify (Captain Shaw) was also in Federal army custody when Davis was being interrogated. Shaw, however, was held as a prisoner of war, not as a spy like Davis. Shaw was later transferred to a Union prisoner of war camp in the north and was released after the war.

When the Davis family heard "by grapevine" that a young spy had been caught and hanged in Pulaski, Tennessee, they feared the worst and requested that a "good friend" (Kennedy) go to Pulaski to "learn the truth." Kennedy was a Kentucky native and relative newcomer to Middle Tennessee prior to the war. According to his own account, he was told, "If it is Sam, do your best to get his body and bring it to us."

Davis' mother gave Kennedy pieces of cloth from her son's clothing to enable identification. Lacking personal familiarity, Kennedy relied on the cloth and general description—and the circumstances of the execution—when claiming the body.

Kennedy obviously had strong ties to the leadership of the occupying army, whether business or personal, for he began his quest by going to the headquarters of General Lovell Rousseau in Nashville to get a written pass for travel through various military jurisdictions. The Davis family apparently knew these connections, since they asked Kennedy for help that could only come through contact with the Union army.

Only two specific references to the Kennedy/Rousseau relationship are known. One refers vaguely to the general's "obligation to Kennedy for kindness received from him before the opening of the war." Another describes Rousseau and Kennedy as "boyhood friends from old Kentucky." In any event, Kennedy got his pass and, with the help of some bluff and bluster, according to his own account, made it to Pulaski.

Kennedy continued to receive Union leadership cooperation, and the body of the spy was quickly exhumed. The identification is recounted as follows:

> *The height, about five feet seven or eight inches, the apparent age…and the slender build all corresponded to that of Sam Davis. To more fully prove his identity, Mr. Kennedy turned back the coat and compared the lining of the gray jacket with the piece given him by Mrs. Davis. They were alike…he unwound the cords of the hangman's cap…and, turning back the cap far enough to disclose the upper lip, marked faintly with the young man's first mustache, he was fully convinced that the body was Sam Davis.*

Inquiring as to the exact circumstances of the capture and execution, Kennedy was given a detailed accounting of the boy's extraordinary conduct and courageous comments during interrogation and prior to the execution. As for the arrest and capture, Kennedy learned that "there was no account of the details of Davis' capture in the army records." The details were "secret."

Kennedy did learn that during the interrogation Davis was asked, "Are you the man our scouts chased so close on the Hyde's Ferry pike last Tuesday that you beat their horses in the face with your cap and got away?" Davis' identity as the individual in this incident was known only to himself and those he had told. The young spy was visibly startled by the question, perhaps realizing the identity of his betrayer, but he refused any comment.

In recounting his experience claiming Davis's body, Kennedy emphasized the deference, respect, admiration and assistance of the Yankee leaders and soldiers when his mission was explained. The message was that even those on the other side of the conflict were deeply moved and impressed by the courage and loyalty of the young spy who refused "to betray a friend."

Kennedy worked in Nashville after the war as purchasing agent for the NC&St.L Railroad. In 1896, he told his Sam Davis story at the January meeting of the Tennessee Historical Society. This initiated the Sam Davis Monument Fund with Kennedy as treasurer.

We define heroes based on courageous, unselfish acts, but such conduct must be witnessed and reported to be recognized and celebrated. Certainly, the detailed and sympathetic reporting by a probable "Yankee sympathizer" willing to lend his influence to relieve the pain and uncertainty of a grieving family accounts, in significant part, for the recognition and legend of "the boy hero of the Confederacy."

Kennedy played one more role in the Sam Davis legend. In 1902, when New York sculptor George Zolnay was commissioned to do the statue of the Smyrna native, which now stands at the southwest corner of the state capitol, he had only written and oral descriptions from which to work. When the initial clay bust was completed, Zolnay—working in Nashville—sought out Kennedy and brought him to his studio without explanation. When the bust was uncovered, Kennedy reportedly exclaimed, "My God—it's Sam!"

Founder's Death and Lynch Mob
Closed Local University

The founder was buried three times, and his successor barely escaped a lynch mob, but the legacy of Union University is still much appreciated—a full city block of "green space" in the center of urban Murfreesboro.

In 1838, the fledgling Southern Baptist leadership decided that a university was needed for educating young ministers. Because it was expected that such an institution would unite the many diverse Baptist denominations in the mid-South, the new school would be named Union University.

Early in 1840, the church leadership opened the school in Somerville, Tennessee, but it was poorly patronized and financed. Seeking a fresh start in a more central location, the school was moved in May 1841 to a dilapidated two-story log structure that had previously housed the defunct Bradley Academy in Murfreesboro. Joseph H. Eaton was appointed president and Latin professor for the new university. To supplement his income, he also became the first pastor for the new First Baptist Church in Murfreesboro.

From the outset, the university finances were precarious, and Eaton spent much of his time riding horseback around the region pleading and praying for contributions. Meanwhile, his wife, Esther, a granddaughter of Thomas Treadwell, a signer of the Declaration of Independence, maintained the household and launched a "monthly magazine for the mothers and daughters of the South and West." Feature articles included "Be Just to Your Stomach" and "Letters to Young Wives." Annual subscriptions were two dollars.

With a pledge of $10,000.00 from the City of Murfreesboro, and a modest treasury accumulated by Eaton, in 1848 the university trustees purchased eighteen rural acres "on the north side of the stage road from Murfreesboro to McMinnville" (now East Main) from Matthias Murfree for $2,121.25. Soon construction began, and in December 1851, the university moved into its new home, a gray brick, three-story colonnaded structure with over twenty thousand square feet of floor space. Outbuildings included two privies (male and female?), a stable for commuting students and eventually a residence for the Eaton family (funded largely by Esther's magazine income). In new facilities, the school quickly reached its zenith.

By 1855, the enrollment was nearly three hundred with a curriculum emphasizing the classics, math and theological texts. Yet there were problems; the faculty began demanding regular payment of salaries, and student disciplinary problems began to spill into the community. (One theology student was killed in a drunken saloon brawl, and two others were shot in a deadly dispute with the local cobbler.) The school also initiated a bitter dispute with management of the new railroad for running pleasure trips and "blowing the train whistle on the Sabbath." (School spokesmen accused the railroaders of being Catholic.)

For all intents, the school "died" on January 12, 1859, with the death of President Eaton at the age of forty-seven. The memorials and funeral were lavish, with church, community and school participation. Soon after burial in the cemetery next to the Baptist church (now the Old City Cemetery), a fundraising was begun for an "appropriate" memorial. A few months later, work was begun on an elaborate tomb adorned with a three-foot figure flanked by Greek urns on the southeast corner of the campus. Before year's end, Eaton's remains were dug up and moved with much fanfare to the on-campus tomb.

For a brief period, the school resumed operations under its new president, James M. Pendleton. Known for his unpopular opinions, Pendleton insisted that he was only "an emancipationist," not an abolitionist, and in fact kept one female house servant. Nevertheless, he fled the area as a Civil War–enflamed lynch mob gathered near the university. (History does not reflect whether he fled with or without his female servant.)

During the war, the abandoned university building was heavily abused and vandalized. Windows, doors and woodwork were used for firewood. Attempts to reopen after the war were frustrated by lack of funds, cholera fears and pressure to move closer to supportive congregations in West Tennessee. On directive from the Tennessee Baptist hierarchy, the name (and little else) was moved to Jackson, Tennessee, on October 10, 1875. The university trustees (mostly Rutherford residents) vigorously opposed the move and retained title to the local property.

For five years, the abandoned university building was used by a military school and other academic projects, but by 1880 it had been abandoned again and deemed unsafe, and the trustees filed a federal claim for war damages. For twenty-seven years the building stood vacant, and the campus became overgrown. Finally, in 1907 the property was given to the new Tennessee College for Women. The new owners, however, did not favor the continued presence of the Eaton tomb, and once again the founder's remains were exhumed and moved, along with his monument, to Evergreen Cemetery.

The local legal entity and its board of trustees were finally dissolved in 1915 after a federal claims payment of $15,000 was transferred to the new Tennessee College. The Tennessee College closed in or about 1940, and the

The last of three graves for Union University founder. *Photograph by Kevin G. Tucker.*

new Central High School was built on the property in the mid-'40s. The Central Middle School now uses the eastern two-thirds of the old university property. The western one-third is today a popular open area for a variety of public and private activities.

Many Roles for North Maple Street Property

When the church moved from its first home on North Maple, most of the churchyard graves were also moved, but a number of the deceased continued to lie beneath the cotton gins and, later, beneath the feet of the "southern magnolias," the Tigers, the utility linemen and the public employees.

In 1811, a popular Methodist evangelist held a series of camp meetings around Rutherford County, reportedly converting hundreds to this increasingly popular protestant faith. It was not until 1823, however, that the first Methodist church was established in an appropriate structure in Murfreesboro. The lot purchased by the congregation was on the west side of North Maple in what is now the 400 block. (In 1819, this lot was used for the county gallows.)

This early church was built of brick sixty by forty feet, plastered and painted, with a box pulpit and bench seats. On the south end of the property was the church cemetery. But by the late 1830s, the congregation had outgrown this structure, and in 1843 the church moved to a new building on the corner of Church and College Streets. In connection with the move, the original church site was sold, and "a majority of the bodies buried (in the church graveyard) were disinterred and reburied in the city cemetery," according to C.C. Henderson in *The Story of Murfreesboro* (1929). Less than half were apparently left behind and abandoned. (In most jurisdictions during the nineteenth century, graves were generally considered the responsibility of the surviving family. If there was a reason for relocation, it was up to the family to complete the task. If there was no family, or if the family had not the means or the interest, the grave sites would simply disappear.)

The church property was sold to Thomas Robertson, who installed equipment and workspace for the manufacture of cotton gins. In 1851, Robertson sold the property to the trustees of Soule College, a Methodist-affiliated school offering "a traditional southern education for women in cultural studies and social graces." The old church/factory building was demolished, and a three-story, Classic-style facility, 135 feet by 115 feet, was erected for the school.

Except for the Civil War period, the school grew and prospered through the second half of the nineteenth century. (After the war, the school reopened with an announcement that there were "no school marms from the North...all Southern magnolias.") Soule reached its zenith at the turn of the century when Virginia O. Wardlaw and her sister, Mary Snead, headed the school. These two names were "synonymous with distinction in education in the South." The two educators were described as "brilliant…women of fine character and gentle demeanor."

In 1903, the two sisters bought the school from the church-affiliated trustees and then added to the school faculty and administration two more sisters, their mother, two nephews and a niece. Soon, there was trouble with rumors of occult and other strange activity. Enrollment and finances plunged, and in 1907 the Wardlaw/Snead family left the area, leaving the school to new owners. Under new leadership, the school recovered its image but was never again a financial success, in part due to competition from the area's new Tennessee College for Women and the new Normal School. (Wardlaw and Snead relocated to New Jersey and, in 1910, were the focus of a sensational national scandal involving a mysterious bathtub drowning, homicide allegations, suicide, narcotics abuse and a Murfreesboro bank lockbox full of diamonds. But that's another story.)

The last Soule graduation was in 1917, several months after the property was sold to the City of Murfreesboro for construction of a modern Central High School. The city paid $4,000 for the campus property and demolished the old school building. The new Central High School building was completed in 1919 with "an auditorium seating one thousand, a gymnasium with seating for four hundred, and a library of two thousand volumes." During the 1920s, the school was "graded A1 by the State Board of Education, a distinction held by but five schools [out of five hundred] in the state," according to a contemporary *Handbook of Rutherford County*.

In the 1920s, the home at the northern boundary of the school grounds was occupied by James A. Moore. According to local historian C.B. Arnett, Moore was at the time reputed to be "the only infidel in Rutherford County." Aggravated by high school students coming onto his property, he enclosed his yard with a stone and brick fence, part of which still stands.

Twenty-five years after its completion, the home of the Central High Tigers was destroyed by fire. The school was rebuilt on East Main, and the Maple Street property remained vacant until the Middle Tennessee Electric Membership Cooperative (MTEMC) bought the property and built its new office and operations facility in 1951. A half century later, MTEMC moved to new headquarters on New Salem Road and sold the Maple Street property to the Murfreesboro Housing Authority, which now occupies the former utility, high school, female college, factory, church, graveyard and gallows property.

II

THE GREAT DEPRESSION

POND DIGGING FOR A DOLLAR A DAY

In 1933, in order to "put the populace back to work" in the depths of the Great Depression, the new Roosevelt Administration created a number of public works programs. Among these was the Civilian Conservation Corps (CCC), which put young men to work on forestry, conservation and other outdoor projects.

The CCC set up base camps and tent camps in rural and undeveloped areas across the United States and recruited young, able-bodied men with the promise of food, board, hard work and the attractive wage of one dollar a day. The Rutherford County base camp was on property that is now the back lot for Alexander Chevrolet. Permanent structures were built for housing, feeding and schooling. Drives and walkways were lined with hand-cut limestone blocks, many of which remained in place until just recently. John Hendrix, a sixteen-year-old CCC recruit in 1938, remembers that stones marking the site were still in place five years ago but have since disappeared.

Joe Halliburton led the local group, Hendrix remembers, and Ira Daniels was one of the instructors. Another veteran, Carl Gilbert, recalls that Edgar Preston, James Helton and Jim Jenkins were among the Rutherford natives who joined the CCC. Willie McElroy and "Red" Victory were also among the CCC boys.

John David Hendrix (left) and several CCC colleagues spend their free time in front of a CCC cabin in the Murfreesboro camp in 1938. *Photograph from the collection of John David Hendrix.*

CCC recruits were taught outdoor, building and landscaping skills. Hendrix recalls classes in welding and blasting, but when crew leaders discovered that he was an enthusiastic and relatively good cook, he was assigned to the cooking crew with a baking specialty.

Gilbert and Hendrix worked on CCC crews that built fire towers, cleared roadways, planted trees, crushed rocks for lime and roads and dug farm ponds. But no matter what the project, at 3:00 p.m. on Friday of every week, the entire crew was taken to the Stones River milldam near Manson Pike for "tool washing."

Clayton Faulkner, as a teenager in the Donnells Chapel community in the mid-1930s, remembers when the CCC built a large pond just east of the Cripple Creek Road "for the benefit of the local farmers needing to water stock during dry times." It was located on property then owned by Clarence Denton across the road from the Charles Youree farm.

The CCC was not funded for heavy equipment, so the pond was hand dug with picks and shovels and finished off with hand rakes. "We did have a mule and a big pond scoop," reports Hendrix. The CCC boys were not always experienced or schooled in the "science" of their projects, and they worked often by trial and error. But they apparently understood the task requirements when they built the Donnells Chapel pond, for it held water. They knew not to bottom it on bare rock and were careful to line it with clay subsoil. The locals don't remember whether the CCC used farm animals to "season" the pond bottom. (There is a consensus among senior stockmen in this area that you should pen pigs in a new pond before it begins to fill with water. The pigs will "root out" all of the organic matter, and their droppings will seal the soil, making the pond watertight. Some of the old-timers believe that cattle will do just as well, but according to Kittrell-area farmer and trapper Wayne Reed, quoting his father, the pigs are a "sure thing.")

The senior Guy James was chairman of the local CCC committee and screened applicants during the Depression. Ralph Fullerton's father was CCC camp commander in Kentucky. There was a dance party every Saturday night for the camp boys and their dates. Fullerton, then about eight years old, was in charge of the record player for those parties.

CCC work was apparently a great conditioner for a young man. Hendrix went from the CCC to military service during World War II and then returned to Rutherford County as a lineman for MTEMC (Middle Tennessee Electric Membership Corporation). He retired from the utility after forty years of service and then ran a one-man lawn-care service for another decade. His colleagues recall that he was known for his strength and had the strongest grip of anyone working the lines.

Weather Pilots and Barnstormers

With the first regional airport opening here in 1929, Rutherford County figured prominently in the early history of commercial aviation in the southeastern United States, and the aviation industry added a number of colorful personalities to local folklore.

In the 1930s, Sky Harbor, on what is now the Old Nashville Highway near Florence Road, was the major airport serving the southeastern states, with Anderson Airways (later renamed American Airlines) operating daily passenger service flying the Curtiss Condor.

The airport also served as the National Weather Service base for the region, and young Frank Knapp was one of the weather service pilots.

BECAUSE SKY HARBOR was the major regional airport in the southeast, many coast-to-coast and Midwest-to-Florida flights landed here for rest and refueling. Frequently, celebrities were aboard. The late Ed Lowe remembered meeting Clark Gable, Errol Flynn, David Niven and several "Hollywood beauties." Harris Dement recalls hearing that Will Rogers landed his plane at Sky Harbor but stayed in the plane to avoid the crowd that had gathered. Dement also reports that Charles Lindbergh flew mail into Sky Harbor.

Sam Woods believes that pilots followed the railroad to find the airport. Woods attended the opening program at the new airport in 1929. Word was spread that Charlie Given would make a parachute jump. A biplane circled, and out came the jumper, but the chute didn't open and the daredevil hit the ground with a loud "thud." It was a dummy, not Charlie.

John McDonald was on the Saturday morning scene shortly after the Curtiss Condor missed the runway and crashed across Florence Road in 1936. He carried home a piece of the plane as a souvenir. Several passengers, including the pilot, were injured, but all eighteen survived.

Sky Harbor closed as an airport just prior to World War II because the newer planes required more runway, and Sky Harbor, between the Nashville Highway and the railroad line, was unable to expand. Because early airmail service relied on the railroads to complete delivery to areas away from air terminals, the Sky

Every morning, Knapp or one of his colleagues would crank up a single-engine biplane (probably a Curtiss P6E Hawk) and climb to maximum altitude (about twenty-five thousand feet) to take various temperature and atmospheric readings for the weather service. Their equipment was rather limited and primitive even for that period. The high altitude and unpressurized cockpit required that the pilot use oxygen, so the pilots flew with a manually operated air tank connected to a rubber tube that they clenched in their teeth. The breathing equipment was home-rigged from whatever materials were available. At various elevations while ascending, they would read the weather instruments, hand write the data and suck oxygen through the rubber tube. After landing, they would give their data to a base operator, who would transmit it to the central weather service office.

One morning in the mid-1930s, a local schoolteacher driving to work along Florence Road noticed a small plane hanging in the upper branches of a large oak tree near the airport. After several hours' work, rescuers finally got Knapp out of the plane wreckage and into ground transport to the hospital. He was treated for multiple fractures and trauma, which only a fit young man in excellent health could survive. After over a month in the hospital, Knapp returned to his weather service job. Although he never was able to recall or explain what had gone wrong during his near fatal flight, others speculated that he may have dropped the oxygen tube and passed out.

Knapp continued to be active in local aviation and eventually served on the Metropolitan Airport Authority Board in Nashville. The road to the general aviation hangars at the Metro airport is named in his honor.

But not everybody who flew into Sky Harbor in the 1930s was involved in commercial aviation or working for a government program. Some, like Bowser Frakes, a Columbia, Tennessee native, were pure entrepreneurs. During the first four decades of powered flight, a number of private daredevils toured the countryside putting on "air shows" for local communities where airplanes were still a novelty. They were in it for the money, and Frakes was a local "barnstormer" in the purest and most literal sense.

For his performance finale, Frakes would dive his wood and fabric craft through a barn or other convenient building—in one door and out the other side with

Harbor location was initially believed to be ideal. Ten years later, the physical boundaries forced relocation to a site in Davidson County.

O.T. Ridley Jr., son of the Sky Harbor manager who was responsible for the original airport construction, attended the grand opening and dedication of the facility in 1929. "I remember that Jimmy Doolittle was there and did a handstand on the hand railing of the new terminal," says Ridley. At the time, Doolittle was a popular stunt pilot. Later, he was credited with developing instrument flight. Early in World War II, Doolittle bolstered American confidence by making a daring bombing raid on Tokyo.

Former LaVergne mayor and postmaster A.C. Puckett remembers barnstormers. "Airplanes were such a novelty that hundreds would come out just to see a plane in action." In 1930, in Lincoln County, Puckett's family went to a nearby pasture where plane rides were being given. The pilot decided to "buzz the crowd to scare them back off the field" but came in so low he actually struck some of the curious onlookers. Puckett's father took several to the hospital in his Model A.

Some of the airport structures were dismantled in the 1960s. Ed Jordan recalls buying several of the old structural timbers. They were two by twelve (actual measure) and twenty-seven feet long. "As I remember, I paid six cents a foot. We nailed them together and made feeding troughs," says Jordan. "When I sold the farm forty years later, they were still in use."

Curtiss P6E Hawk, one of several biplanes used by weather service pilots in the 1930s.

Air show at Sky Harbor, circa 1930. *Both photographs from the collection of Ed and Kathleen Lowe.*

only the fuselage and tail gear intact. The plane wings would be knocked completely off the plane as it entered the building. Frakes had, of course, rigged his wings with shear pins and pull rings so that they would come off on first contact while he rolled through the barn, hopefully unscathed in the cockpit and fuselage. Understandably, Frakes always required that his performance fee be paid in advance in cash.

During the mid-1930s, an air show was being staged at Sky Harbor as a fundraiser for the local Red Cross chapter. Frakes was hired to do his barnstorming act. On the day of the show, the organizers had second thoughts and concluded that a mangled pilot in the wreckage of the airport hangar and plane would not be a good image for the Red Cross. That risk, plus the potential financial liability for property damage, persuaded the show organizers to cancel the performance by Bowser Frakes.

Frakes made no objection; he just flew home with the Red Cross cash in his pocket.

Our late regional aviation master, G.E. Lowe Jr. of the Blackman community, remembered both Knapp and Frakes, for he was witness to all of the foregoing events.

CAMP MULLYWATT ONCE SERVED RUTHERFORD BOY SCOUTS

Some of the Scouts called it "Camp Mullywatt," remembers Guy James Jr. The name was never official and may have had some connection to the electrical element of the camp's origin, but most folks just called it the Boy Scout Camp.

Boy Scout groups in Rutherford County today operate under official charters issued by the Boy Scouts of America Middle Tennessee Council, based in Nashville, which holds the "franchise" from the national organization for all of the counties in Middle Tennessee. But this was not the way things were organized in the 1930s, when the Boy Scouts of America was growing rapidly in membership and popularity, despite Depression-era funding problems. The Nashville organization had little reach beyond Davidson County.

Scout leaders in Tullahoma organized their own scout council in 1928, called the Davy Crockett Council, and built Camp Fisher, a scout

Art from the Scout Annual *(1937).*

summer camp on the Duck River near Manchester. Scouts from Coffee, Bedford, Franklin, Grundy and Rutherford Counties used Camp Fisher, and St. George Jones and Professor Baxter Hobgood from Murfreesboro were among the camp leaders.

Thomas B. Cannon IV was one of the Boy Scouts from Rutherford County who spent weeks at Camp Fisher in 1931 and 1932. "We swam above a dam on the Duck River," recalls Cannon. "I earned my swimming merit badge there." Thomas A. Moore, a Murfreesboro insurance agent, was the camp director.

Encouraged by the activity in Tullahoma, Rutherford scout leaders also organized an independent Boy Scout council with local resources and facilities. One enthusiastic and influential volunteer scout leader in Rutherford during this period was Clarence Watson, head of local operations for the Tennessee Electric Power Company (TEPCO). (After the forced merger of TEPCO into TVA, Watson headed the Murfreesboro Power Department.)

Watson understood that scouting meant camping, and in the early 1930s he was determined to build a summer camp for the boys in Rutherford County. His quest and negotiations settled on a hillside area overlooking the Stones River East Fork near the old Browns Mill. This relatively remote site was ideal in part because of the swimming and fishing opportunities in the old millpond.

The site was part of the five-hundred-acre farm belonging to Guy James Sr. Watson and James were friends, and the scout leader asked the farmer if something could be arranged so the scouts could use part of the farm. At that time, this eastern portion of the county did not have electricity, and James was willing to strike a deal. If Watson would bring electricity to the farm, the scouts could set up their camp.

It wasn't long before electric lights were on in the James home and milk barn, and work was underway on the camp. "They built a big central lodge with a huge fireplace and a screen porch overlooking the river," recalls Guy Jr.

Art from the Scout Annual *(1937).*

"There were also eight or ten cabins or lean-tos for the scouts." In 1933, the first summer camp program was conducted at Camp Mullywatt.

Although Guy Jr. was only nine years old (scouts had to be at least twelve), he camped out for the first night with the first group, which also included the Watson boys—Eddie and Billy. They raised and saluted the flag, swam, fished, hiked, cooked over fires, slept on the ground, dug latrines, sang and told stories around the campfire. B.B. Kerr and the Tucker boys, Tommy and Burney Lee, were among the scout campers during the early years, and B.B. Gracey was one of the scoutmasters.

Following World War II, the Nashville scout organization merged with the smaller scout organizations in Clarksville (Cogioba), Tullahoma (Davy Crockett), Columbia (Middle Tennessee) and Rutherford County and assumed the name originally used in Columbia: Middle Tennessee Council, BSA. The Nashville organization also offered summer camping at Camp Boxwell (originally near Linden, Tennessee, and later at the Narrows of the Harpeth River in Cheatham County) to all Boy Scouts in Middle Tennessee.

After the mergers, scout use of Camp Mullywatt declined, although the site continued to be a popular venue for civic, church and private groups through the 1950s. Fire destroyed the lodge in the early 1960s, and the camp was forever closed. "Lightning may have caused the fire," says Guy Jr.

In 1990, the James family sold the former campsite and farm to the county. The site was approved for a landfill, but the landfill operation was never initiated. Recently, the land was transferred to MTSU. The old campsite is now part of the beef cattle farm and teaching facility operated by the university.

DEPRESSION-ERA FOLKLORISTS FEATURED RUTHERFORD SNAKES

During the early Depression years, the Works Progress Administration (WPA) put skilled artisans, tradesmen and laborers back to work building and rebuilding infrastructure, restoring historic sites and completing similar projects requiring manual skill and heavy labor. These projects offered little opportunity, however, for those in the fields of art, music, drama and literature. As part of the New Deal program intended to create jobs in these fields, the Federal Writers' Project was enacted in July 1935 to provide work for unemployed teachers, newsmen, ministers, poets and publishers.

In Tennessee, the project leaders began with ambitious plans to develop a dozen or more publications on state history, handicrafts, Sequoyah (Cherokee alphabet), state parks, floods, horse racing, soil conservation and folk tales. But when funding ended in 1941, only two manuscripts had achieved publication: *Tennessee: A Guide to the State* (Viking Press, 1939) and *God Bless the Devil* (University of North Carolina Press, 1940).

The latter is a collection of "liars' bench tales" edited from numerous sources by the last project administrator, James R. Aswell, a Nashville native and former newsman. Among this collection is one story specifically taken from Rutherford County sources. In the book's preface, Aswell wrote:

> *Every small county seat in Tennessee has its Liars' Bench, a gathering place for the local historians, yarn-spinners and wags. In the heat and good fellowship… talk for the pure sake of talking blossoms at its most extravagant.*

The Rutherford story, personally documented by Aswell, appears to have assimilated several tall tales about snakes from several local sources. The tale is presented in the vernacular, as it was originally heard. Reproducing and preserving the vernacular style was an express purpose of the project. Aswell explained:

> *Much of the effectiveness and distinctive flavor of* [these] *stories lies in the vernacular of the teller. It is a vigorous idiomatic speech, deep-rooted in the past…* [where] *a man freely uses verbs as nouns, nouns as verbs, adverbs and adjectives as nouns, or puts them to any other unorthodox task he chooses.*

The attempt to phonetically reproduce the dialect of the rural Middle Tennessee storyteller of the 1930s may be difficult for the contemporary reader, but the abridged portion of the Rutherford tale, "Snake Country" that follows is true to the original:

> *Dis use to be snake country…In my young days man couldn't hardly walk from de house to de barn widout…jumpin an bouncing up and*

Art from God Bless the Devil *(1940).*

down less he want his laigs all chaw up by de snakes. Hit wawn't nothing to see snakes jes hangin by de hundreds off tree limbs like wash on de line.

Hard to keep cows dem days. Too many milksnakes round here. Dem milksnakes…hang around de pasture lot jes waitin faw de cows' bags to fill up wid milk. Den right smack up de cow's left hind leg go de snake an grab hold and start suckin faw who laugh de longest. Wouldn't turn loose…till [the cow] *look faw a fact like some ol dry rag.*

One day we looks around for the cows. Dere dey stands chawin dey cud…but dem bags! Jes little old dried up nothins!…I looks around [and] *sees dem hateful ol milksnakes…all swol up wid milk to de bigness of a fat man's laig, layin up sound asleep. Well, I didn't do nothing but hang up dem sleepy ol snakes by dey tails,* [and] *milk dem snakes from de tail down to de haid. Ol milk jes come foamerin out an fill de buckets…So from den on we never fool wid milkin no cows. We jes milk de snakes.*

One day back yander there was a regular siege of stingin snakes…dey was devils. Pizen at both end, in de bite an in de sting…But de good Lord never put nothing bad on this earth dat he didn't put something else good to cure hit. If you's stang by one of em, you go let a rattlesnake bite you an dat kill de sting pizen. If you's bit by tother end of a stingin snake, why de pizen of a copperhaid cure dat. When anybody go out dey tote two fruit jars round dey neck wid couple of copperhaids an rattlers in dem case de party got stang or bit by de stingin snakes. So nobody round dere got kilt by dem rascals.

Then der was de year de graveyard snakes was sech a pest. Dey's big fat ol white snakes dat lives in graves. Ain't got no bite aw nothing to kill a man, but you hates to have em round you count of where dey hangs out an de way dey smells like a six-day cawpse.

Course when you crosses a snake's track, hit give you de hot miseries in yo back less you walks backwards over dat track. Dey was so many snake tracks in dem days dat it was mighty slow to git anywhere. Man starts out faw Smyrna. Every step he take he have to back-step. Fo dat man know hit, he done back his self back clean to Murfreesboro. An if he bound for Murfreesboro, he land in Smyrna. So if a man want to go to Smyrna, he better haid for Murfreesboro. Hit was pretty slow dem days…ain't no telling how hit come out if something hadn't happen.

One day bright and early de snakes started leavin de county. Yes, snakes by de tens an thousands. De come pilin out of de hills and bottoms till hit look like they gwine cover de earth. De hit de roads goin west, wigglin an workin three foot deep. Hissin could be heard for miles. Dey stirred up a dust dat darken de sun. By [next day] *hit wawn't a snake in dis county ceptin de lame, de halt, and de sickly. Faw a time hit was a puzzle, but finely folks figger why all dem snakes left. Seems like dey's SOME folks round here wawn't satisfied wid stickin to the hard down cold facts bout snakes…dey begun makin up LIES about de snakes. So de snakes jes got mad an up an left de county.*

SCOUT HUT BREAK-IN WAS A SURPRISE FOR SCOUTMASTER

Soon after the Murfreesboro scouts broke in through a window at 702 Ewing Boulevard in 1967, work began for the lawyers and thespians.

In the mid-1930s, First Lady Eleanor Roosevelt became concerned that the various New Deal work programs (Works Progress Administration, Civilian Conservation Corps, etc.) were not reaching poor, urban youth (ages sixteen to twenty-five) who were unskilled and educationally disadvantaged. Accordingly, she personally advocated the establishment of a National Youth Administration (NYA) to provide educational and work opportunities for targeted youth groups.

Few were surprised when the influential first lady got what she asked for, and the NYA was initiated and funded in June 1935. The federal agency defined programs and distributed funds but left program initiation and management to state control. According to State of Tennessee records, NYA employees "built vocational and recreational buildings all over Tennessee, including workshops and Boy Scout lodges."

Among the first in Rutherford County to see a potential community benefit from NYA building projects were Dr. W.T. Robison and B.B. Gracey Jr., leaders in the local Boy Scout Council. They negotiated a tentative commitment from the NYA leadership to build a "Scout hut" contingent on finding an appropriate site where the structure could be built and dedicated to scout use "in perpetuity."

On January 13, 1938, the Murfreesboro City Council, Mayor W.A. Miles presiding, reviewed a request from the scout leaders that the city "donate to the Scouts a vacant lot on Ewing…on which the Scouts may erect a hut for their use." The requested property was lot 76 in the Harrison-Black Addition, a residential development just west of the Normal School (now MTSU). The 80- by 176-foot lot had been acquired by the city for $140 in January 1930 as part of a waterworks project. It was one of five subdivision lots between Ewing and Bell Streets acquired for installation of a steel water tower, but as finally constructed, the tower and related facilities did not use lot 76. (Gracey was apparently quite familiar with the property. Deed records show that he had bought and sold the property just a few years earlier.) The request was referred to an ad hoc committee for study and recommendation.

Two weeks later, the committee reported favorably on the request and recommended referral to the city attorney to work out the details and draw up the necessary papers. On motion from T.J. Dement, the recommendation was approved unanimously. It took the lawyers twenty-one months to "work out the details," but finally on October 19, 1939, the city council approved a deed giving the scouts a permanent easement on lot 76 with the city retaining title. The conveyance was actually to C.E. Watson, J.C. Mitchell, St. George Jones and Leiper Freeman, and their successors, as officers of the local Boy Scout Council.

Within a year, the NYA completed a rustic, two-story log house with a full basement and wraparound porch. The first floor was a large open area for scout activity. Equipment storage was in the basement, and the second floor was partitioned for small group meetings. For the next twenty-five years the structure was used by various scout groups, despite leadership and organizational changes in the local scout program. (In the 1940s, the local Boy Scout Council was dissolved, and local troops became part of the Middle Tennessee Council based in Nashville.)

By the 1960s, the structure had been redesignated as the "Scout Lodge" and was home to Troop 359 with Percy Dempsey as scoutmaster. Among the scouts were Ewing Sellers, Larry Tolbert, Jim Garner and Bob Corlew. Now serving as Rutherford County chancellor, Corlew remembers that the Flaming Arrow and Eagle Patrols met in the upstairs rooms, and bonfires were sometimes built in the backyard. "Weather permitting, we would often play softball in the Jaycees Park beside the water tower."

A special occasion was the surprise fiftieth birthday party for Scoutmaster Dempsey in 1967. "The lodge was locked when the scouts weren't meeting, and Mr. Dempsey had the only key. In order to decorate and set out food without giving away the surprise, we jimmied open a window," confesses Corlew. "And since all the doors were padlocked and couldn't be opened from either side, all the parents and guests, as well as the scouts, had to crawl through the window. The food, decorations and everything else had to be passed through this forced opening." Corlew remembers in particular helping his mother crawl through the window. "I just never would have thought of my mother sneaking in through a jimmied window, but in the scouts we had a lot of new experiences."

The current Log Cabin Playhouse next to the water tower on Ewing Boulevard in Murfreesboro was built by a Depression-era work project for the local Boy Scouts. *Photograph courtesy of the* Daily News Journal, *Murfreesboro.*

When Scoutmaster Dempsey arrived early to unlock for the evening program, he was by all accounts "surprised."

But repair and maintenance (including roof and plumbing leaks) were major concerns in 1967, and the scout leaders in Nashville, technically the easement owners by succession, were not willing or able to fund renovations in Murfreesboro. Dempsey and other local leaders, including Jim Burkhalter, Roy Fairbanks and Ken Bumpas, eventually agreed to a partnership with the Murfreesboro Little Theatre (MLT), an amateur theatre group that was looking for a more suitable venue for its programs. Attorney Richard LaRoche was retained to resolve the complexities of the federal program mandate, the easement ownership and the city title.

In 1968, renovations funded through MLT efforts enclosed the porch and covered most of the exterior logs. "It was originally planned that the scouts and MLT would share the facility," remembers Corlew, "but the MLT modifications hampered the scout activity, so the scouts eventually decided to use other facilities."

Now officially designated as the Log Cabin Playhouse, the old Scout hut is leased from the City of Murfreesboro by MLT through at least 2020.

A Depression Odyssey

One-Lunger Cadillac Offered Depression-Era Relief

Newton Wright, grandson of Edward F. Wright of Wright's Spring Mill in the Halls Hill community, remembers hearing about how the old doctor would boast that he was the first sawbones in Tennessee to sell his horse and buggy and start making rounds in a motorcar. The doctor was probably "extravagating" (that's a Halls Hill term), but his vehicle was just about as early an original as was ever seen in Rutherford County.

Making his rounds through the Kittrell, Sharpsville, Halls Hill, Porterfield and Milton communities before and after World War I, J.D. Hall, MD, drove his 1903 Cadillac, for which he or a predecessor had paid the impressive sum of $750. Built a year earlier and first marketed in 1903, this "one-lunger" was the first production-model Cadillac.

Henry M. Leland, a Detroit manufacturer of marine engines in the 1890s, organized the Detroit Auto Company and hired young Henry Ford

J.D. Hall, MD, with his wife and Cadillac. *Photograph from the collection of Dalton Stroop.*

EARLY ORDERS ARE NECESSARY

IF YOU DESIRE TO POSSESS A

Cadillac...

A LOOK OUGHT TO TELL YOU WHY

It's as good as it looks and will sell for $750.00. Complete with tonneau, $850 00.

The agent who doesn't secure it NOW, is apt to hie himself to the woodshed a little later, and gently kick himself all over the place.

Will you be one of the unfortunates? Now is the time to decide.

CADILLAC AUTOMOBILE COMPANY

DETROIT, MICH.

WILLIAM E. METZGER, Sales Manager

This 1902 advertisement encourages early auto dealers to order the first production-model Cadillac. One of these early vehicles has an unusual Rutherford County history.

as his chief engineer. Although the two Henrys clashed over questions of engine design and Ford was fired before the first car was sold, it is generally acknowledged that the first Cadillac models were developed by the young engineer. (Dash oil lamps, tail lamp and horn sold separately.)

The 1903 car was powered by a gasoline-fueled, one-cylinder engine with a flywheel and chain drive. It was crank started with a side-mounted hand crank, had one seat centered on a classic carriage-style body and was durable to a fault. (The one-cylinder engine with its "huff-and-puff" rhythm prompted the "one-lunger" nickname.)

But even this durable Cad was ready for retirement after nearly twenty years on the dirt and river-gravel roads of Rutherford County's eastern frontier. The doctor sold the car, and Ed Wright eventually acquired it "as is" for ten dollars. The car was parked on the creek bank next to the mill to be "cannibalized" as needed. It was just a season or two later that the creek flooded, part of the bank washed out and the one-lunger settled on the bottom of the channel.

Six or eight years later, twenty-three-year-old Frank Wright, younger son of Ed Wright, known locally as "Frankie T," was repairing an old Buick when he remembered the car in the creek as a possible source of parts. He and his buddy Ellis Floyd fished the old Cadillac out of Cripple Creek, and after some tinkering and cleaning decided it was more interesting than the Buick.

The year was 1930, the Great Depression was settling in for a long stay and Frank and Ellis had been out of work since the sawmill closed. Odd jobs were as rare as full-time employment, and the young men found some promise, or at least some distraction, in the mechanical dinosaur salvaged from the creek.

After many hours of repair and mechanical improvisation, the engine was once again producing power. All of the wood and fabric body was long rotted away, so they rigged a single seat in the middle over the engine, mounted a box on the rear and made a small platform on the front. A "new" radiator was fashioned from other project remnants. While one drove, the other could ride high on the rear or sit below the level of the steering wheel on the front.

Now began the adventure—first to Murfreesboro! In the spring of 1931, a Murfreesboro daily newspaper headlined: "Auto, 25 Years Old, Comes From Kittrell Here." The *Journal* reported that the car had driven from Kittrell "in little more than a half hour, a distance of nine miles." According to the report, the car "chugging its way around the square, 'hitting on all ONE,' created quite a bit of excitement."

The occasion for this first road trip—Frank driving and Ellis riding up front—was a gathering of Civil War veterans at the Confederate memorial on the square. Speculating as to the reason for the unexpected appearance of the old Cadillac, the newspaper said: "Maybe it was here in honor of the Civil War veterans who well remember when such vehicles were known as 'gas buggies' and when folks said it was a sin to drive around at the terrific speed of ten miles per hour."

Encouraged by the Murfreesboro reception, and by the attention attracted on a subsequent drive to Nashville (including an offer to trade a new Ford for the vintage Caddy), Frank and Ellis decided to drive to Cadillac (GMC) headquarters in Detroit to solicit perhaps an even better offer. At the speed of twenty miles an hour, they expected to make the northern trip in about ten days.

They left Murfreesboro on Wednesday, June 3, and on Saturday, June 6, were featured in word and picture on the front page of the *Cincinnati Post* under the headline: "Look Out, We're Tearing Along on All One!" The *Post* reported that "Frank and Ellis are on their way to Detroit in hopes that the car manufacturer will hire them." Ellis is quoted as saying, "We don't want a lot of money…just a job. We think the company that made this auto might give us a job just driving the car around the country."

The *Post* explained that the one-cylinder auto gets about fifty miles to the gallon of gas "if the road is level" and can go as fast as thirty miles per hour "but gets pretty hot so you have to stop and cool her off." The faint smell of alcohol from the homemade radiator mounted above a rear wheel also prompted comment in Cincinnati.

As expected, the folks in Detroit were very curious about the car, but there were no job offers. Disappointed but undaunted, Frank and Ellis next headed to Chattanooga, where they drove up on Lookout Mountain, and then swung through north Georgia and down to Atlanta. At every stop, the car would draw a crowd. Now they were beginning to understand and recognize the commercial potential of the old car—sideboard advertising for local businesses…and maybe "the movies."

Halls Hill One-Lunger Went Coast to Coast

With an abundance of youthful confidence, Depression-era joblessness and an offer from the *Rutherford Courier* to provide some gasoline money in exchange for written travel reports, Frank Wright and Ellis Floyd began preparing for their westward odyssey in August 1931.

The 1903 one-cylinder Cadillac was readied for its coast-to-coast trip with a false radiator, rear seat and toolbox. The actual radiator was a milk can with a distillery coil and hose mounted over the left rear axle. *Photograph from the collection of Newton Wright.*

Their 1903 one-lunger Cadillac, rescued from its watery grave and tested on trips to Detroit and Atlanta, was now readied for a Halls Hill to Hollywood run. A second seat was added over the rear axle, and a false radiator front was installed with an oversized Cadillac logo and the "Standard of the World" motto. A boxlike structure behind the radiator front proclaimed "Coast-to-Coast!" A toolbox was secured to the rear.

On August 10, 1931, the *Rutherford Courier* reported that the old Cadillac was heading west.

> *Wherever the car goes, put-putting along the road, it draws much attention… Many take snap shots of the old machine that a country doctor used near a generation ago, and no doubt the people gathered around it in those days and marveled that a machine could go thirty miles an hour never imagining that they would see the day a car would travel 60 miles an hour along great ribbons of concrete roads.*

Promoting reader interest in the Cadillac journey financed in part by the newspaper, the *Courier* continued:

And now this same machine is of much interest to the people of today as years ago, but how different the interest—today its antiquity holds the mind…a generation ago its speed held the imagination of those who thought it the acme of service and speed.

The first travel report appeared on page one of the *Courier* on August 13 from Little Rock, Arkansas: "We are now past the mosquito infested swamps of the Mississippi and in the fine little town of Little Rock." The newspaper elaborated:

Frank Wright and Ellis Floyd, who have the oldest "cadillacking" Cadillac in the world, are capitalizing this fact by using the old car to travel over the United States as a living advertisement on the long life of this make of automobile.

The next report was from Texas:

We have made it through Arkansas and across Texas to El Paso. We start the 24ᵗʰ across New Mexico, temperature 140 degrees on the desert. Our lips and part of our faces were blistered by the wind while crossing Texas. We are ready for the worst part. We are advertising here for five days.

Whenever they came to a town, Frank and Ellis would try to sell advertising on the old car to the local Cadillac dealer. They approached service stations offering to swap advertising for fuel. Local movie theatres were their next best market. They would remain in a town long enough to run out any ad contracts and raise enough spare cash and fuel to get to their next stop.

Temporary housing was usually part of any advertising agreement, but sleeping often meant a barn or on the ground. With many homeless itinerants during the Depression, roadside camps were common, and some of the displaced were willing to share what little they had. Others would steal. Violence was not uncommon. The Rutherford adventurers were friendly, naïve and lucky. Perhaps the focus of attention and curiosity on their vintage car afforded some protection.

On September 12, 1931, Frank wrote from Hollywood, California: "How's the depression back there? Write and tell me all about it." Staying in the home of a cousin, Charles Jetton, Frank reported on the last leg of their westward journey:

> *Well, made the trip all right. We had an accident on top of Rocky Mountain one night when a wheel of the old Cadillac ran off as we were coming down the mountain. Ellis was riding on the back seat and he fell off and slid for about 20 feet—wore all the hide off his pants. It surely was some experience coming off there at night while making about 40 per. It was all I could do to hold the car in the road…We had to wait until morning to find our wheel.*

The reception in Los Angeles included enough local fanfare to raise hopes for a lucrative visit. The arrival of the rare vehicle and its "intrepid endurance heroes from way down south" was reported in the *Los Angeles Examiner* under the headline "Multi-Stop Flight Across US in 1902 One Lung Auto Ends." A newspaper picture showed the car with a policeman looking and scratching his head. "The people concluded it was a car as it had four wheels," wrote Frank.

Documenting the arrival, the *Examiner* reported:

> *Marking an epoch in transcontinental travel, Frank Wright and Ellis Floyd…were greeted by long lanes of amazed faces and loud volleys of friendly laughter. The journey from Halls Hill…in the Tennessee mountains…*[was made] *in a machine which has come to be known as an automobile.*
>
> *Their endurance crown was won by surviving thousands of miles of cross-country travel in an open air, one cylinder Cadillac at top speed of 20 miles…They plan to spend their first winter in Southern California if they can find work enough to keep their car supplied with gasoline and oil. Driving the car is not as expensive as it is exhausting…it averages from 40 to 50 miles on the gallon.*

Commenting on Hollywood, Frank wrote:

> *People go crazy over our car out here. Nice place to live—if you are rich. I am going to stay out here awhile. About 20,000,000 people—it seems—out here. I got an appointment with a studio; don't know what kind of a pass I will make. I tell everybody about home in Tennessee.*

One-Lunger Starred in Hollywood Comedy

Jobless and restless, two young men from the Halls Hill community rescued a 1903 auto relic from the bottom of the creek, restored the one-cylinder engine ("one-lunger") and headed west in 1931 promoting Cadillac durability and whatever else would help pay their way in the depths of the Great Depression.

Riding open-air on what was billed as the oldest operating Cadillac in the world, Frank Wright and Ellis Floyd attracted crowds at every stop and sold enough sideboard advertising to keep them going all the way to Hollywood. Many people along the way were amused and engaged by the Tennesseans' endurance and enthusiasm and offered aid and encouragement. At a stop in Arizona, a physician asked Frank if he had any "protection." Getting a negative answer from the young adventurer, the doctor gave him an old single-shot, .22-caliber rifle and some advice about avoiding hoboes and gypsies.

The initial September reception in Hollywood was encouraging. The first visit to the Hal Roach Studios prompted a newsreel appearance with the famous Hollywood comedy duo, Stan Laurel and Oliver Hardy, examining the old one-lunger—fun, but no money.

Hollywood prospects looked promising when the Mack Sennett studio leased the old Cadillac for a comic short starring Andy Clyde (best known for his role as the comic sidekick of William Boyd in the *Hopalong Cassidy* series) and a very young Robert Young (later a television star—*Father Knows Best* and *Marcus Welby, MD*). This time there was money and a bonus benefit—the one-lunger got a Hollywood makeover (fenders, side panels, a steering tiller, various accessories and new seats). The film, titled *Speed of the Gay Nineties*, also featured Barney Oldfield as a race car driver. "My car won the race," wrote Wright. "It was called the mystery car."

Now optimistic, Frank wrote home about a possible advertising job that could pay "$25 dollars a day" and finance the trip "back East." They were enjoying California:

> *Went to the Pacific yesterday. Had a fine time. Saw some people catch a young seal; a great crowd was on hand to witness the catch. We see people here from all over the world, and all of them say they have never heard a Cadillac hit like this one.*

But Frank and Ellis soon learned that Hollywood has a short attention span, and further movie prospects were nil. In late October 1931, Frank advised the *Rutherford Courier* that "my buddy Ellis started back to Tennessee

Comic actors Oliver Hardy (standing behind the car) and Stan Laurel inspect the one-lunger Cadillac driven from Rutherford County to Hollywood by Frank Wright (at the steering wheel) and Ellis Floyd.

Hollywood regulars Andy Clyde (left) and Robert Young used the 1903 Cadillac from Tennessee in the comedy short entitled *Speed of the Gay Nineties*. *Both photographs from the collection of Newton Wright.*

Frank Wright from Halls Hill drives his refurbished 1903 Cadillac advertising for the RKO Orpheum theatre in Seattle, Washington, in 1932. In a "Hollywood makeover," the car was fitted with new front wheels, sideboards, seats, fenders, sidelights and fuel tank. *Photograph from the collection of Newton Wright.*

today. I don't know where he will stop to get work. I guess I will stick it out here this winter."

Emma V. Whitworth, daughter of Ellis Floyd, assumes that her father "rode his thumb home." He may have been frustrated with the California prospects and worn out from all the "cadillacking." But most likely, his return was motivated by thoughts of Mollie, for they were married shortly after his return. (A few years later, Ellis bought the old Halls Hill mill and began raising his family in the millhouse, but that's another story.)

Meanwhile, California regulations became an issue. Frank was advised by local authorities that he could not drive the Cadillac around advertising for various clients unless he paid the state fee for vehicle registration. So the 1903 Cadillac became the oldest car registered in California in 1932.

The California girls also were not meeting Frank's expectations:

> *The women out here sure do make me tired. It's a hand full of "give me" and a mouth full of "much oblige." She say: "Ice cream soda and teabone*

steak, if you want to win a woman get a Cadillac Eight." Boy, I believe a Cadillac One will have to do me.

Wright left Southern California in February 1932 and headed north. A letter from Seattle recounted some of the trip:

Here I am in Seattle. Got a job tomorrow with the RKO theatre. I have postponed but few meals, and haven't missed any...I had to get an odd wheel to replace the one I lost in the mountains. Snow was six feet deep in the mountains I crossed. I came near freezing. The only way I could tell the road was the tracks left by others. I almost froze to death on top of the Shasta mountains in Oregon—some state. I slept in my car...and saw some gold miners.

Curious about news from home, or perhaps a bit homesick, Frank concluded, "Please send me a copy of the *Rutherford Courier* to Walla Walla, Washington, general delivery. Yours very truly, Frank Wright, The Tennessee Kid."

Heading East, Cadillac Met Bedbugs, Gypsies, Henry Ford

Now venturing alone in the 1903 one-cylinder Cadillac, Halls Hill native Frankie T. Wright, in the spring of 1932, headed east from Seattle. He planned a northern route down through Chicago and home to Tennessee in the car that had been salvaged from the creek and restored to serviceability by two unemployed victims of the Great Depression.

But after traveling more than three thousand miles across deserts and mountains in heat and freezing weather, the old one-lunger was demanding more and more attention. On April 19, Wright pushed his way into Montana: "After coming through several muddy places, I had to put on my last spare chain. Wore a tire clear out in mud...after pushing up several hills, finally made it to Thompson Station...camped for night and whole town came to see car." Four days later, after another hundred miles, he limped into Deer Lodge with "clutch slipping and bearing wore out."

The kindness of others and the "labor swap" economy of the Depression, however, continued to support the self-named "Tennessee Kid"—"I cleaned off a yard for a lady and she baked a cake for me." With help from locals, he made it to Butte, Montana, on April 25 and had a run of good fortune.

To finance his trip to the West Coast in 1931 driving a 1903 Cadillac, Frank Wright offered to advertise Cadillac durability and local Cadillac dealers. In Portland, Oregon, Wright worked with the Clark Cadillac dealership. He and his one-cylinder car posed with a 1932 Cadillac in front of the dealership. *Photograph from the collection of Newton Wright.*

I've been in Butte for a week. The biggest copper mine in the world is here and the largest smelter…I went down in the mine…queer place. They have a toilet on wheels there. Worked for the Rialto theatre. Last night the Elks had a big parade. Got the old Cadillac in front of it and people sure did give it a hand. Had two axels made.

In Butte, Wright met another young, unemployed wanderer, Bert Tebo, who agreed to "partner" on the Cadillac venture heading back east. At least he could push…and run. While pushing through mud near Billings, the car "got loose and started running down hill," but Tebo caught up with it, jumped in and put on the brake. When Wright left Billings heading east, Tebo hitched a ride west back to Butte.

Following a route across eastern Montana, North Dakota and Minnesota that is today Interstate 94, Wright and the one-lunger stayed in auto camps, which were prevalent in the 1930s for migrants, vagrants and adventurous tourists. Writing at the Elk River Tourist Camp in Minnesota, Wright observed, "Nice place. Lots of shade and nice green grass. Sure is a pretty camp on 10th Highway. Got up at 9…shaved, cooked and ate…sure was a nice place."

But thirty miles farther, near the Twin Cities, he wrote, "Twin City auto camp...lots of bed bugs, no lights, no water, just a couple of bunks and a roof over...Here's hoping the bed bugs leave part of me tonight." Several miles on the other side of St. Paul, Wright wrote:

> *Camped with a bunch of Gipsies tonight. When I drove into camp, they got all over the car. I couldn't stand having about twenty of 'em leaning on the car, so I grounded the spark plug. When I pulled the switch they hollered like they was shot. They got off and I didn't have to tell them to let things alone after that...but I did put up the curtains so they wouldn't see me cooking.*

The spring weather in the far north was also a challenge. On May 15, Wright wrote:

> *Came about 60 miles today. Put in rod bearing. Had trouble keeping it tight. Clutch slipping. It is cold. Wind is blowing about 70 miles a ower... it was ninety in shade yesterday but today is freezing. Camped beside a sheepherders shack tonight. Wind coming round corner is cold. Like to have frozen last night.*

Wright was, however, impressed by the northern countryside:

> *Quite a farming country. Can hear tractors running everywhere. No trees anywhere. Rolling country. Good roads so far. Awful pretty grass, lots of little snakes...sure is beautiful here, everything green. Sun shining, birds singing. Just enough rain to keep the dust down.*

One year and three days after leaving home in Rutherford County, Wright and the "one-lunger" Cadillac arrived in Chicago. After the first night in a hotel, he noted, "Here I am all swallowed up in Chicago. Hope I don't get lost...or shot by all them gangsters. I'm kindly thinking of leaving Chicago tomorrow. Things don't look too hot for me here."

On the following day, Wright resumed his odyssey:

> *I left old Chicago with no bullet holes in me or my car...what a night. Didn't have money for a room so I tried to camp out. If I was in the country, I could sleep anywhere, but just try to sleep in a Chicago park. A cop comes up every time you get asleep and hits you on the feet.*

Hoping to sell the old Cadillac, Wright headed back to Detroit and the Cadillac factory. The Cadillac personnel remembered his visit a year earlier and were amazed and amused by his travel tales but offered no chance for a sale and a train ride home. Knowing that the 1903 Cadillac had been originally designed by Henry Ford, Wright visited Ford headquarters and met the auto pioneer.

Ford apparently enjoyed the visit with the young Tennessean and the old one-lunger and gave Wright a tour of the Ford museum, airport and plant. He also gave Wright parts for rebuilding the old car's front end. But again, no sale.

On June 13, 1932, Frank Wright wrote in his diary:

> *Today is the thirteenth. I hope it's lucky for me because I'm starting my third trip in the Caddy—Detroit to Reno. I haven't given up yet. I'm going to make good. This is the third try, it ought to take. They are going to have a roundup of old autos and a gold rush celebration (in Reno). I ought to get a prize. I worked the old car over today at a tourist camp. Getting it ready for more miles. Started my misery again. To Reno or Bust! Always, The Tenn. Kid.*

Old Cadillac Finally Got Halls Hill Homecoming

In 1932, as the Great Depression gripped the country and dust storms ravaged the Midwest, two men were crisscrossing America. One was Franklin D. Roosevelt from New York, campaigning for president and promising a New Deal. The other was Frankie T. Wright from Rutherford County, Tennessee, driving a thirty-year-old, one-cylinder Cadillac and looking for *any deal.*

After making the trek from the Halls Hill community to Hollywood, north through the mountain snows to Seattle and east across the northern tier to Detroit, both car and driver were famous for endurance, but fame had not yet led to fortune. Wright was determined to impress all with the engineering and durability of the old one-lunger, to sell it as a museum relic to a "well-heeled" buyer and to return home in style with money in his pocket.

But despite his cross-country odyssey, two Hollywood film appearances for the old car and a scrapbook full of front-page articles from around the country, neither the Detroit-based Cadillac manufacturer nor Henry Ford, the original design engineer for the car, would make an offer to purchase the venerable old one-lunger. Discouraged but still determined, Wright heard

Ellis Floyd (left) and Frank Wright inspect the car that they rode from Halls Hill to Hollywood during the early years of the Great Depression. This photograph was taken in the mid-1970s. *Photograph from the collection of Newton Wright.*

tales of a major old car roundup and celebration soon to be held in Reno, Nevada, and once again headed west. "I haven't given up yet. I'm going to make good."

Crossing the vast dust bowl in late June, however, was hard on both man and machine:

> *Parked last night in Junction City, Kansas. Slept on car seat. There was a knot on the seat, now there is a knot on me. Didn't sleep so much, and I look like Abe Lincoln. Haven't shaved in four days…Think I had about twenty punctures the other day. It sure was hot. Boy, how the sweat rolled.*

On June 20 he wrote, "Have had about 200 punctures in last 1000 miles, and I don't extravagate any."

After coming across the Great Salt Lake and crossing the desert into Nevada, he wrote, "Have had 20 punctures in last two days. Like about 250 miles into Reno…I'm fixing a puncture now."

Wright arrived in Reno on June 29, 1932, three weeks before the auto round-up. He bargained for a couple of "new" used tires, found a free place to camp and felt a renewed optimism and confidence. "Going down town now to see what I can do," he wrote. "Have got pretty good rubber now. I guess I will get a divorce from the old Cad here." Later that evening, he continued, "Went down town. Saw the gambling houses. Never saw so much money at one time in my life. It was just stacked up in silver dollars. I couldn't begin to count."

His diary entry two days later reads:

> *Have not got anything lined up yet. I can write a little better now cause I just went around to the post office and got my pen filled. Boy, they sure are stingy with ink in those ink wells...I postponed three meals since getting here, but I just got filled up at a restaurant...I'm so full I can hardly write. I've started out rite on the first of July. Here's hoping everybody luck.*

But there was no luck in Reno for the self-styled Tennessee Kid, and there was no more waiting around for the auto round-up. "Six days is a long time to stay in Reno," he wrote on July 4.

> *They call it the biggest little town in the world. I agree with them if they will put in the biggest little HOLD UP town in the world. I ain't writing down nothing I can't back up. You would be surprised at what I found out about the Roundup here...a lot of hokum. If your going west, detour Reno.*

Wright and the one-lunger left Reno on July 6 heading north through central California. For the next five months, the odyssey took them into Canada and over the Mexican border. Wright survived on sideboard advertising revenue from movie houses and car dealers, on contributions from garages and gas stations and on occasional handouts of food and shelter. "Out of grub," he wrote one day. Two days later, he noted, "Camped last night at a fellows house...Let me stay in his basement. Gave me a pair of springs to sleep on. Went down to the Ashoated gas company this morning and he gave me 6 gallons to burn."

Finally, in December 1932, the Murfreesboro newspaper reported on the Cadillac's return.

> *Frank Wright, who has fittingly been dubbed the "Tennessee Kid" hove into home Monday riding in his nationally famous "one-lung" flivver...after*

Remains of the Wright Mill, where the one-cylinder 1903 Cadillac was salvaged from Cripple Creek in 1931. *Photograph from the collection of Newton Wright.*

---

touring the states in all ways and directions, covering a distance of about 30,000 miles, chugging from place to place, in the movies of Hollywood, the snow of Seattle and the mud of the Northwest.

Robert Stroop remembers the homecoming. A crowd of thirty or more gathered at Sam McElroy's store at the top of the hill. "Pretty much all the neighbors in Halls Hill," recalls Stroop, "including Ellis 'Louse' Floyd [Wright's companion when the trip began in August 1931]." There was much excitement when the cloud of dust was sighted on the gravel road from Murfreesboro. "Someone shouted 'Here he comes!' and everybody cheered," says Stroop. "Then we listened to his stories and ate baloney sandwiches."

But the one-lunger was not yet ready for retirement. In August 1933, Wright and his car were contracted to make a tour of the South from New Orleans east promoting Pan American Petroleum products. Thereafter, the car was a common sight around Rutherford County, and many of the next generation remember playing on it. "Some of the car parts disappeared during World War II army maneuvers," remembers Newton Wright, son of the Tennessee Kid.

Today, the remains of the original one-cylinder Cadillac rest in a Manchester, Tennessee backyard. The engine, flywheel and chain drive are still intact. After examining the remains, Ralph Puckett, an authority on cars of that era, observed, "Wouldn't be too hard to get it running again."

III

World War II

Tragic End to Local Mining

If you need brass, then you need zinc. During World War II, the demand for brass peaked because of shell casings and other wartime requirements. In the 1930s, Tennessee was aggressively explored and developed by mining interests encouraged by the overseas wartime demand. Most of the activity was in East Tennessee, but there was a known deposit of relatively high-quality ore extending from the hills north of Milton to just east of Readyville.

For almost fifty years, local geologists had been aware of a significant outcropping of zinc ore on the Floyd Knight farm near the Wilson County line north of the Milton community. Located on the headwaters of Bradley Creek, the ore vein outcropped on the creek bed about two hundred feet southeast of the old barn. (Remnants of the mining structures are still in place around the flooded mine shaft.)

The ore vein was discovered in 1889 and first worked in 1895, when two investors (Dickerson and Doyle) sank a shaft seventy-six feet. At that depth, they were overwhelmed by water, which gushed into the shaft faster than pumps could handle. The shaft filled so rapidly that the miners fled up the shaft, leaving their tools behind. The investors abandoned the project in 1904.

No other work was attempted until 1937, when Dr. Gant Gaither from Hopkinsville, Kentucky, began efforts to pump out the old shaft. Encouraged by rising wartime prices, Gaither finally pumped the shaft dry by putting a

The ore bucket that brought an abrupt end to area zinc mining is now a garden fixture in the Donnells Chapel community. *Photograph courtesy of the* Daily News Journal, *Murfreesboro.*

sump pump at the bottom of a two-hundred-foot "churn hole" drilled in one corner of the old shaft. To maintain the dry shaft, a new tractor-driven turbine pump was set up to clear about 150 gallons of "strong sulphur water" per minute. The original nineteenth-century tools were found at the bottom of the old shaft.

The shaft was eventually deepened to 145 feet with two lateral branches. A five-hundred-pound bucket hoist was installed and run by a small "donkey engine," according to a 1951 state inspection report. When the pump occasionally failed, the shaft would quickly refill, and it took three days to again dewater.

Mineworkers went up and down the shaft riding in the bucket. Ore and waste material were removed from the shaft in the same bucket. (Bucket remnants recently found on-site appear to have been hand-formed. What remains of the mine bucket now serves as a flower box in the Donnells Chapel community.)

In the 1940s, zinc ore from the Knight property was trucked to a processing facility near Readyville. Dr. Gaither also owned mineral rights at this Cannon County site—called the Hoover-Carter mine—with a shaft that reached the end of the ore vein at about 150 feet.

In 1947, there was a fatal accident at the Knight mine. A mineworker, a Milton community native, was killed when he fell from the bucket. As a result of this accident, Dr. Gaither was no longer able "to secure insurance protection and as a consequence had to close the Knight and Hoover mines," according to a state geologist report.

Mineral rights on the Knight farm were recently extinguished, and those for the Hoover-Carter site may have also lapsed or been extinguished. We wonder, however, if the continuing run-up in mineral values will ever again make it profitable to work the only known zinc deposits in Middle Tennessee.

BILLY HARRELL OF Leanna remembers when his family took a Sunday drive in or about 1946 on the church bus, with his uncle driving. "We went to see the zinc mine on North Milton Road. It was in operation at that time, and I remember that they had a Buick Straight-8 engine set up to run the mine bucket lift."

HOMELAND PREPARED FOR AIR RAIDS

Since the terrorist attack on the World Trade Center, we have all felt less safe and have accepted the burden and restraint of "homeland security" procedures. Is this an unprecedented period of American insecurity reaching even to our doorsteps in Rutherford County? Perhaps not.

In 1942, the *Daily News Journal* assumed responsibility for distribution of a leaflet with the heading:

VALUABLE!!
(Place This Leaflet Up PERMANENTLY for Ready Reference)
AIR RAID INSTRUCTIONS

The leaflet advised that a bell in the courthouse would be the air raid signal and indicated that each outlying community should implement some similar kind of alarm. The leaflet further instructed that when the signal is heard, everyone should "keep calm and cool...stay home—don't stampede...put out all lights...lie down if bombs fall...stay away from windows...do not telephone."

As for personal protection of life and limb "if explosive bombs fall near," the local population was instructed to "keep mouth open by placing a rolled

VALUABLE!!

(Place This Leaflet Up PERMANENTLY for Ready Reference)

AIR RAID INSTRUCTIONS

WHEN YOU HEAR THE AIR RAID SIGNAL:

*(A bell in the court house dome in Murfreesboro—
a signal will be devised later for other communities)*

1. Keep calm and cool
2. Stay home—don't stampede
3. Put out all lights or screen windows so light will not show
4. Lie down if bombs fall nearby
5. Stay away from windows
6. Do not telephone
7. If away from home—
   (a) Stop car—extinguish lights
   (b) Walk, don't run, to the shelter the Auxiliary Police or Air Raid Warden assigns you.
8. Turn off gas stove burners but not pilot light—If gas line is damaged report it to Air Raid Warden.
9. If explosive bombs fall near, keep mouth open by placing a rolled handkerchief between teeth—protect ears with hands—protect back of head—don't look up—lie down under heavy table or davenport and relax.
10. If Incendiary bombs fall, watch attics and upstairs rooms for bombs.
    (a) Leave bomb alone for the FIRST MINUTE (60 seconds) as it may be an explosive type.
    (b) Handle with sand, bucket and shovel after this time has elapsed.
    (c) Use water to put out the fire started by the Incendiary bomb. DO NOT PUT WATER ON THE INCENDIARY BOMB AS WATER WILL EXPLODE IT if not properly applied.
    (d) If a garden hose is available SPRAY water on bomb to increase exhaustive burning.
11. Appoint a "warden" for your house to remember all the rules and train family to obey them.
12. Stay in doors until the "all clear" sounds. (Usually the same signal as the air raid alarm)
13. Obey your warden—conditions may change from time to time and his instructions are official.

Above All Be Calm and Cool

SUGGESTED MATERIALS TO HAVE ON HAND:

1. 50 pounds sand.
2. Long handle shovel.
3. Buckets to contain 10 gallons of water.
4. Flashlight.
5. Garden hose.

Approved by Murfreesboro and Rutherford County Civilian Defense Council

COMPLIMENTS OF

TELEPHONES
22 or 38

The Daily News Journal
RUTHERFORD COUNTY'S HOME NEWSPAPER SINCE 1848

MURFREESBORO,
TENNESSEE

handkerchief between teeth—protect ears with hands—protect back of head—don't look up—lie down under heavy table or davenport and relax." (Might be difficult to relax while biting a rolled handkerchief and hiding under a davenport as bombs explode!)

Special procedures were given for incendiary bombs:

> *Leave bomb alone for the FIRST MINUTE...Handle with sand, bucket and shovel after this time has elapsed...Use water to put out the fire...DO NOT PUT WATER ON THE INCENDIARY BOMB AS WATER WILL EXPLODE IT...If garden hose available SPRAY water on bomb to increase exhaustive burning.*

(This probably required some practice and concentration!)

The leaflet also indicated that each household should have on hand "50 pounds sand, long handle shovel, buckets to contain 10 gallons water, flashlight, and garden hose." (Is that two five-gallon or five two-gallon buckets?)

Home defense was a very serious concern even before the surprise attack on Pearl Harbor. By November 1941, 5,935 U.S. cities and towns had set up defense councils and trained air raid wardens. After the Japanese attack, nearly all of the approximately ten thousand cities and towns established such procedures. City and town blackouts, intended to prevent targeting by enemy bombers, were practiced. The wardens were charged with enforcing civilian compliance during the blackouts.

Grady Miller was one of several wardens in Murfreesboro. R.A. "Bobby" Huddleston Jr. recalls that his neighbor, Warden Miller, wore an official armband showing his authority. Mrs. Miller embroidered an armband for then ten-year-old Bobby. "I would tag along with the Warden to see if any outside lights were on or if light was showing around the blackout shades and drapes in windows," remembers Huddleston.

In hindsight, the fear of a World War II bombing raid on Rutherford County strikes us as irrational, but in 1942 this was all deadly serious—just like the "duck and cover" school drills of the 1950s and the stockpiling of food and medicines in public building bomb shelters in the 1960s. Could it be that every generation must prepare for the worst that current events can suggest? We can only hope and pray that the next generation will shake its collective head in wonder over the irrational preparations and anticipation that were part of "homeland security" fears in the early twenty-first century.

Fortunately, we still have the *Daily News Journal* for "Ready Reference."

"Too Old, Too Young, Exempt or Deferred"

Tennesseans "too young, too old, exempt or deferred" could meet their "patriotic duty" by volunteering during World War II to serve without pay as members of the Tennessee State Guard. According to official records, the members were "recognized as soldiers under the authority of the U.S. Constitution" and Tennessee law.

Anticipating war with Germany, in September 1940 the Roosevelt administration "federalized" all National Guard units, including the 30th Division in Tennessee, which was mustered into active duty in preparation for European combat in February 1941.

Even before the federalization, Tennessee leaders recognized how grim things were looking and, in May 1940, became the first state to set up a civilian state defense organization. In 1941, this organization was renamed the State Defense Council with retired Adjutant General T.A. Frazier as chairman.

Governor Prentice Cooper believed that in the absence of the National Guard, a replacement military force was needed in Tennessee, and he signed Chapter 15, Public Acts of 1941, to create such a force. Under the State Defense Council, this was to be an "adequately trained force for employment within the boundaries and jurisdiction" of the state. The General Assembly appropriated $500,000 and authorized the governor to use other "emergency funds" as needed to ensure that the state guard was able to act when needed to "maintain laws, meet domestic emergencies, guard and protect vital industries, suppress the activities of enemy agents, and cooperate with Federal authorities in extreme emergencies." In particular, the Tennessee Guard was charged with protecting the TVA system.

Once again, Tennessee justified its reputation as the Volunteer State. Even before the Tennessee State Guard was one year old, it was the largest guard unit in the South and the largest in the nation in proportion to state population. It was the first state guard to receive federally supervised field training and was equipped and trained before most other state units got beyond the first stages of organization. State Defense Council chairman Frazier reported in mid-1943 that the state guard was "thoroughly disciplined and conditioned to endure hardship with high morale" while repelling invasion, quelling domestic disturbances or committing sabotage in the event of enemy occupation. (Frazier also saved the old University of Nashville building from demolition by making it his headquarters.)

The "too old, too young, exempt or deferred" filled the ranks of Company L of the Tennessee State Guard in 1943. Captain R.A. Huddleston, commanding officer, is on the left in the front row. *Photograph from the collection of Robert Huddleston Jr.*

The Second Brigade, headquartered in Nashville, included all of Middle Tennessee. Company L in Rutherford County was part of the Second Regiment, also based in Nashville. The ranking officers were mostly World War I veterans. (The Seventh Regiment based in Cookeville was commanded by Colonel Alvin York.) George L. Osborne originally headed Company L in Rutherford County, but shortly after the start of recruiting, Osborne resigned and Governor Cooper commissioned R. Alvis Huddleston as captain and commanding officer of the Rutherford unit.

Huddleston had served in France with the 306th Signal Battalion, 81st Division, during World War I and was in the Argonne when the Armistice was signed. He was also a former commander of the local American Legion Post and active in the local business community as a realtor and insurance agent. Officers serving under Captain Huddleston included First Lieutenant Franklin Pearson, Second Lieutenant Henry Alexander and First Sergeant Cecil Elrod Jr. Pearson and Alexander were field artillery veterans, and Elrod was a graduate of the Georgia Military Academy. Henry C. Moore III was the company clerk.

Company L was the first occupant of the new Armory built on Nashville Pike (still in use today as the county garage, waste collection offices and emergency management base). Work on the Armory was completed using county workhouse labor. Pending completion of that facility, Company L conducted unit drills each Tuesday night at the Training School (predecessor of MTSU). Equipment authorization for the state guard units included rifles, submachine guns, shotguns, ammunition, armored cars, ambulances, reconnaissance vehicles and trucks.

Although trained, equipped and ready, Company L never repelled invaders or sabotaged an occupying enemy, but it did guard a military aircraft crash site, maintain the peace during a labor dispute in Anderson County and quell a deadly race riot. On February 26, 1946, the *Daily News Journal* reported that Company L had been "alerted just before midnight…and spearheaded the State Guard advance into Columbia (Maury County) at 3 AM." According to state records, Company L "dispersed a crowd of whites who were congregating at Columbia's Mink Slide." One observer recalled that when the armored vehicle pulled up in the middle of the street and pointed the gun at the threatening crowd, the riot ended. Thereafter, on orders of the governor, Company L searched every house and business in the Mink Slide (Columbia) community and confiscated all firearms. (Apparently, neither the ACLU nor the NRA raised Second or Fourth Amendment objections.)

The state guard was officially deactivated on January 1, 1948.

MOUNTED CATTLE DRIVE A RARE, DUSTY WARTIME EXPERIENCE

In 1942, as the United States shifted to a wartime economy, Joe L. Montgomery moved his young family from Macon County to Rutherford County. The small, family farm near Red Boiling Springs could not support all of the Montgomery clan, and Joe was hoping for better circumstances sharecropping on a large Halls Hill farm owned by Sterling Wall.

Sharecropping arose after the Civil War and was still common throughout the Southeast into the 1950s. At the end of the Civil War, many Southern farmers had ample land but no cash for wages. At the same time, many former slaves and impoverished small farmers lacked the means, skills or opportunity to be self-supporting. The solution was the sharecropping system. The "cropper" brings to the farm his and his family's labor. All other requirements are provided by the farm owner or landlord.

In return for his labor, the cropper gets housing on the farm property and a share of the farm income. From this share, the landlord may deduct credit advanced to meet the living expenses of the cropper's family. The system was common in Rutherford until farm mechanization made farming less labor intensive, and the postwar economy offered more work opportunities.

After two years, as one of six sharecropper families on the Wall farm, Montgomery moved his family to what promised a better return as the only sharecropper on a Lascassas Pike farm. The farm encompassed what is now the Garrison Cove subdivision and was owned in 1944 by the Pearson family. Bill Pearson managed the farm for his mother and also managed a thousand-acre farm owned by his father-in-law, "Uncle Tom" Elam, in the Big Springs community. (This farm was later purchased by Opry stars Jim Reeves and Jimmy C. Newman. The latter performer still lives on about five hundred acres of the original farm.)

In 1945, Pearson decided to move a herd of cattle from the Lascassas Pike farm to the Big Springs property. War rationing was still in effect, and hiring a truck or trailer was not an option. Pearson decided to drive the cattle across the county "on the hoof." The sharecropper was assigned to go ahead of the herd in the farm pickup, while Pearson rode lead on horseback. Two Montgomery boys, Ray and Comas, were assigned to ride sweep and chase strays.

The drive began early one morning heading out Lascassas Pike across Bushman Creek, then south

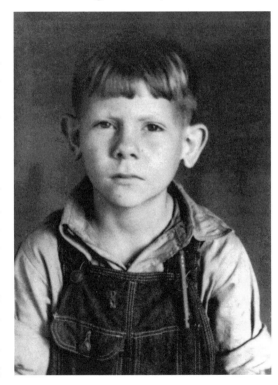

Comas Montgomery. *Photograph from the Montgomery family collection*

on Twin Oak, a winding gravel road, and through rough country past Walnut Grove Church and Bushman Cave. "Most of the roads were gravel, and we ate a lot of dust riding behind the herd," remembers Comas, then a twelve-year-old. "Cattle would head off the road down farm lanes or driveways, and we would have to chase 'em and turn 'em back. That was the fun part."

The drive crossed Halls Hill Pike west of the Shiloh community. The pickup had stopped at the intersection, as planned, to control the traffic, but there was no traffic. "I don't think we passed a car on the whole trip," says Comas. (Unessential driving was considered unpatriotic during the war, and gas and tire rationing, plus a thirty-five-mile-per-hour national speed limit, made most driving impractical.)

"I remember we turned onto the Woodbury Pike at the Little Brown Jug," says Comas. (The Jug was a popular college hangout in the years before and during the war and continued as a local tavern under the same name until the 1990s. Billy Burch, who caught the pass that beat Tennessee Tech for the STC Homecoming in 1940, observed recently, "If you had a quarter, the Jug was a good place to take your date—two cokes and three plays on the jukebox. It was even better if your girl had the quarter.")

The herd was driven east on the pike to Double Springs Road, just west of the Jakes Town community. "We let them drink at the pond below the first spring," remembers Comas, "and then we pushed 'em back on the road and went down Double Springs to Veal Road." As they drove through the rural community along Veal, a number of children ran out to the road fence to see the "cowboys." "We tried to put on a show," confesses Comas. He and his brother would "whoop and holler and snap our rope whips whenever we chased a stray or saw somebody watching us."

But the best part of the drive was provided by Leonna Montgomery. "Mama gave each of us a sack of homemade biscuits with homemade sausage and blackberry jam," explains Comas. "Nothing tastes better than Mama's biscuit and blackberry jam eaten on horseback."

The herd was turned on Bradyville Pike at the intersection just south of the Harrell/Todd farm. "By now the cows were tiring and more cooperative, so we made good time out the pike to Lowe Road, where we turned right to go around the big hills," Comas recalls.

"Lowe Road took us right to the farm lane." Exhausted after a full day in the saddle, the Montgomery boys were rewarded with a ride home in the back of the pickup, and for each a seventy-five-cent tip.

"Things changed rapidly in Rutherford after the war," muses Comas, "and I expect that was the last cross-county cattle drive."

New Car Dealers Sacrificed in
Wartime Production

Current pleas from domestic auto makers for government help is a reverse of 1941 circumstances following the attack on Pearl Harbor when the government needed the resources of the American auto industry to prepare for war.

Exercising extraordinary "war powers" in December 1941, the Roosevelt administration initially ordered that only "blackout cars" without chrome and reflective trim could be manufactured and delivered by American automakers. After a furiously paced month of wartime bureaucratic reorganization and departmental shuffling, the new Wartime Production Board ordered that all passenger car production end without exception on February 10, 1942.

Thereafter, the might of the American auto industry led the "production miracle" that transformed the United States into the best-equipped and most formidable war machine in the history of conventional warfare. But such an effort involved many sacrifices, and new car dealerships throughout the country were among the most conspicuous. Many simply disappeared, although some struggled along, dealing in used cars and repairs until rationing and exhausted inventories frustrated even those efforts.

Rutherford County was no exception. Before the war, new car showrooms locally had offered Chevrolet, Buick, Marquette, Oakland, Pontiac, Willys-Knight, Whippet, Chrysler, Dodge, Plymouth, Nash and Ford models. By mid-1942, inventories were depleted, and some of the dealers had disappeared forever. Notably, Earthman-Wilson Motor Car Company (Ford), Wright Motor Company (Nash), Overall-Cook Motor Co. (Packard), Rutherford County Motors (Plymouth and DeSoto) and Hirsbrunner & Miles (Chrysler, Dodge and Plymouth) did not survive.

The war ended, finally, in 1945, and the Truman administration abruptly shut down the "war machine" and returned auto industry resources to private control. At best, industry retooling required at least twelve to eighteen months, and "new" passenger cars were not again available until the fall of 1947. One of the first dealerships to reopen in Rutherford County, after being gone for five years, was the C.R. Byrn Motor Company, reclaiming its status as "Murfreesboro's oldest car dealer" (since 1913).

Charlie Byrn, returning from army duty, reopened the family business in a new location at 125 Front Street, offering Chrysler and Plymouth models on November 7, 1947. The company offered a "complete line of Mo-Par parts" with Gulf Oil products and Johnny C. Lyell as service manager. The grand opening of the Byrn dealership featured a mileage-guessing contest for a twenty-five-dollar prize (a Chrysler car was set to run on jacks from 11:00 a.m. to 6:00 p.m.).

Ford appointed a new dealer for Rutherford County. Robert Weatherford, the son of an established Ford dealer in Munfordville, Kentucky, was a U.S. Navy veteran and a Georgia Tech graduate before accepting the Ford appointment. The grand opening for the new Weatherford Motor Company was on Saturday, December 20, 1942, and featured a "Radio Jamboree" starring Bob Jennings and the Monarch Eagle Rangers. There was a prize drawing for a fifty-dollar U.S. bond, free Princess movie tickets "for the kids" and free refreshments. Bob Coleman was the service manager for the new dealership, which also offered Esso oils and gasoline in the 600 block of West Main.

In this same period, Murfreesboro Motors (a prewar Ford dealer) opened as a Packard dealer on South Academy with D.C. Bryant as manager; Ed Morris Motor Company began selling Studebaker on East Vine; Roy Byrn resumed new car sales of Buick and Pontiac at 212 North Maple; and Nelson-Campbell offered the Kaiser-Frazer on Main Street.

As competition renewed, the focus was often on claims of postwar engineering and design versus simply a new look for prewar models. Studebaker, sporting a new aerodynamic look, boasted "the best by far with a post war car." Buick claimed a newly engineered "Fireball" engine on a prewar body and chassis. "Only Kaiser-Frazer builds genuine post war cars," claimed the Nelson-Campbell dealership, "the result of engineering and design progress made since 1941."

One survivor on West College, Jackson Bros., candidly conceding that the "new" Chevrolet was simply a repackaged prewar model, promoted its car as "the lowest cost." Despite the country music and theatre ticket promotions, the new Ford dealer was also struggling with basically a prewar model, and Weatherford's problems were further complicated by his "outsider" status.

Not all the 1947 start-ups survived, but by 1952 auto retailing was again thriving in Rutherford County with eleven new car dealerships offering fifteen different American nameplates. Weatherford, however, was back home in Kentucky, and the Ford dealership at 621 West Main was locally owned and operated as the Binford-Kearney Motor Co.

War Blunted Revenge of the
Locker Room Rats

Those who were involved still call it the "Revenge of the Locker Room Rats," but it was a moral victory at best, since few remained to enjoy the spoils.

Male day students who lived at home and commuted to the Murfreesboro campus at State Teachers College (now MTSU) in the late 1930s and early 1940s were assigned lockers in the basement of the gymnasium (now the E.W. Midgett Building). The intent was to provide space for temporary storage of books and other personal items during the school day. The result was a hangout and center of activity for the local boys from around Rutherford County. The few crude benches did not limit locker room appeal for lunch and socializing.

Virtually all of the regulars packed their lunches. Brown bags were in style largely for reasons of economy. Another attraction was the shower, for a number of the boys came from homes still without running water.

The daily socializing prompted a group identity, and eventually the locker room regulars began referring to themselves as the "Locker Room Rats." Acknowledged ringleaders in the fall of 1941 were Fred "Hopalong" Cassity from Murfreesboro; Donald Knight, Craynor Elrod and Ralph McKee from Milton; and Ed Loughry from Lascassas. Others from Murfreesboro included James and Jack Harney, Eldridge Tipps, Burney Lee and Tommy Tucker, Ralph and John Hitt, Eph Hoover, Bill and Claude Shacklett, Grady Todd, Cecil Schuler, James Lane, Gentry Brandon, Delbert Driver and Julian "Bud" Lytle. J.W. Reeves, Haywood Hall and Dalton Stroop were from the Sharpsville/Halls Hill area. Gerald Jordan was from Fosterville. Dewey Pedigo and Royce Davenport came in from Woodbury, and Eris Read and Grover E. Maxwell were Rockvale natives. Joe McCrary was from Readyville. William Ross and Silas Coleman carpooled from Smyrna. Roger Smith and Rol Brown drove in from Overall. James Buchanan was from Gum, Willie Dunaway lived in Leanna and Ed Hildreth commuted from Watertown.

Football was a favorite conversation topic during Rat gatherings, and several of the STC team standouts—Eph Hoover, Burney Lee Tucker and Roger Smith—were among the Rats. From these conversations came the idea of entering a float in the homecoming parade, an annual event and competition sponsored by the student government. Campus organizations would enter parade floats of their own design and construction. An impartial panel of judges would select the winner based on creativity and appearance, and the winning organization would be recognized with a cash award during halftime of the homecoming game.

The homecoming opponent in 1941 was Memphis State College, and their mascot was a tiger. After some intense locker room brainstorming, the Rats agreed on a float theme: the STC hillbilly tiger hunter. It was decided that the float would roll on an open jalopy owned by Dalton Stroop and that Bill Ross from Smyrna would be the hillbilly character. Ross had previously been the subject of national media attention as "the barefoot punter." He was a walk-on for STC and participated in preseason practices but never played in a game. "He didn't take very well to discipline," remembers Stroop. Nevertheless, standing six feet, four inches and shoeless, he was a natural for the hillbilly role.

The car was fitted with a platform and a big, weathered barn door. Ross was dressed in cut-off overalls and carried an old-fashioned shotgun. Efforts to obtain a tiger skin were unsuccessful, but a mountain lion skin was borrowed from Cato White (a junior from Lebanon whose father had bagged the lion on a hunt in the Rockies). The lion pelt hung on the barn door. To save on gas, it was decided that the car would be pushed along the parade route, and a dozen Rats were recruited for the push team.

Decked out in school colors and appropriate signage, with Ross mugging and acting out his role and twelve students (including Dill, Jack Harney, Hildreth, T. Tucker, R. Hitt and Dunaway) providing power, the Rats float was a crowd favorite. The parade went west on Main Street from the campus to the county courthouse. The "pushers" were rewarded with a car ride back

to campus, and word soon got around that the Hillbilly Hunter float was the unanimous choice for the top award.

That afternoon, the homecoming football game was a close victory for STC. As recorded in the 1942 *Midlander* (the school annual): "For the homecoming crowd the Raiders won out 13–12 with Hodges and Bain scoring and Tucker kicking the winning point." The halftime program, however, was a disappointment for the Rats. Their float was disqualified from competition because the Locker

Room Rats were not a campus social or academic club recognized by the Associated Student Body (the student governing body). There would be no cash award, no picture in the school annual—nothing.

Not long thereafter, the Rats hatched their plan for revenge: they would seize control of the student government (through democratic means, of course). Using the Rats' many athletic, academic, social and club contacts, they nominated one of their own, Grover Maxwell, for student body president. The Rats printed leaflets and "talked up" their candidate. In the end, it was a landslide victory for Maxwell and the Rats.

But Maxwell did not assume his post when the next school year began. By September 1942, Maxwell and most of the Rats, like thousands of other young men, had answered the call to military service. Among those who did not return were Rat veterans J.W. Reeves, Roger Smith and Eldridge Tipps.

Pilot Skill Avoided Monkey Wrench Disaster

There was literally a monkey wrench in the works. Disaster was averted, but one mechanic lost his job.

For a decade ending in 1939, Sky Harbor on the Nashville Highway just north of Florence Road in Rutherford County was the major airport serving the southeastern United States. Mail, passenger and freight planes flying Chicago to Florida, Washington to California or New Orleans to New York would stop at Sky Harbor for fuel, rest and servicing.

In 1938, however, it was decided that the landlocked facility (built between the highway and the railroad) could not continue to meet the needs of an expanding industry. A new facility was opened a year later near Nashville (the current Air National Guard base is on the original site). The mail service and the passenger airlines abandoned Sky Harbor for the new airport in Davidson County.

Two years later, the nation was preparing for war. The navy and army air corps were training thousands of new pilots. Most of these trainees got their first airplane ride in a single-engine, two-seater biplane designed by Lloyd Stearman. Variously identified as the PT-17 (primary trainer), NS-1, N2S, Boeing Stearman Kaydet or simply "the Stearman," this plane was the most widely used trainer of the war years.

This official U.S. Navy postcard shows three Stearman aircraft flying in a three-plane formation. Ed Lowe mailed the card to his wife in Murfreesboro from flight training school in 1943 using military "free" mail privileges.

Many war-era pilots remember the Stearman as a reliable airplane with finely balanced controls, a strong airframe and a powerful seven-cylinder engine. (After the war, many Stearman were used for aerobatics and crop dusting.) But the high center of gravity, coupled with narrow landing gear and limited forward visibility, created a tricky plane to handle on the ground.

As would be expected, the training activity took its toll on both pilots and aircraft. In 1941, a government contract for repair of the trainer planes was awarded to Air Utilities, Inc. This company moved into the empty Sky Harbor buildings with offices in the old terminal and shops in the empty hangar. A number of local craftsmen were hired, including Herschel Mullins and Ed Lowe.

Mullins was in the watch repair business on the square in Murfreesboro and was anticipating military enlistment in 1941. Skilled workers were needed to repair the instrument panels for the wrecked trainers. When the Air Utilities manager offered employment, he explained to Mullins that the work would be similar to watch repairing and would provide deferment from military service. Mullins closed his shop and took the job.

Although still a teenager, Lowe knew as much about airframe construction as anyone in the country in 1941. His father had been the maintenance and operations chief for Sky Harbor. Lowe (who thought little of formal schooling) had literally grown up in the airport shop. He was hired by Air Utilities as an airframe mechanic and reassembled wings, doped canvas and mended fuselage damage. Lowe rebuilt Stearmans for two years before joining the navy as a pilot and airplane mechanic.

The damaged planes were brought to the shop by train. "The railroad had a spur track for the airport," remembers Mullins. When the planes were again flight-ready, they were flown out in three-plane formations.

"The hangar where we worked burned down about halfway through the war, and for awhile we worked in some sheds at the end of the runway," said Mullins. When the planes took off, they headed straight into the windows of the sheds. It was exciting to see the repaired planes taking off but always a bit scary from where we were." The hangar was rebuilt on the original foundation. The company name was added above the big doors, and the shops were relocated.

Before any plane was returned to service, it was flight-tested from the old Sky Harbor runway. The company had its own test pilot. "I never knew his full name," explained Mullins. "We all just knew him as 'Giles' the test pilot."

Mullins remembers one day in particular when Giles took off on a test run and something went wrong. "We all knew there was a problem because immediately after takeoff he circled low and came back over the field yelling and gesturing to the ground crew."

Mullins heard the shouts but could not understand over the engine noise. "I learned later that the tail controls had jammed, and Giles was telling the ground personnel to get water buckets in position in case he crashed on landing and the plane caught fire."

Giles was a skilled and coolheaded pilot and was able to bring the plane down in one piece. "He landed with the tail up high. It dropped about the time the plane rolled to a stop." As Giles climbed out and others came running up, he said, "Don't anyone touch that plane until I have finished looking it over!" Mullins recalls that the pilot soon determined that someone had left a hand tool, a monkey wrench, in the tail section. On takeoff, the wrench slid against some of the control wires or levers and jammed the controls. "When they figured out who was responsible for the tool, he was fired," remembers Mullins.

As the war ended, military flight training in the Stearman ended. Air Utilities shut down its local plant, and Mullins reopened his watch shop.

This was not, however, the last of Rutherford County's role in the history of the venerable Stearman.

After a long and distinguished career in air safety and airplane engineering, the late Ed Lowe returned to Rutherford in 1970 and started Stones River Air Service, the first private company to operate on what had been Sewart Air Force Base. Owned and managed by Lowe and his wife, Kathleen, the firm restored and maintained planes—including several old Stearmans—for many individuals, agencies and companies.

Lowe kept in his shop a Stearman wing as a "template" for use in restoring the internal structure of a damaged wing. Thanks to the generosity of the Lowe family, the wing is now part of the collection at the Discovery Center (a children's hands-on museum) in Murfreesboro.

As for Air Utilities, Inc., it was sanctioned in 1946 for labor law violations (maybe the wrong mechanic was fired). A successor company today repairs and services helicopters in Newberg, Oregon.

CULPEPPER WINNER BECAME TIRELESS
WALNUT HULLER

The year was 1941, and Dalton Stroop, a Halls Hill native, was finishing his third year at Middle Tennessee State Teachers College (later MTSU) and looking forward to a summer job measuring crops for compliance with government-mandated crop allocations. (As part of the New Deal farm subsidy program, farm production was regulated through federal allotments that specified limits on tobacco and cotton acreage and subsidized certain forage crops.)

For this work, Dalton needed transportation, so he negotiated purchase of a 1928 Chevrolet from Schiele Johnson, a tenant on Sterling Wall's farm in the Halls Hill community. It looked pretty rough, rusty and rotted, with no roof. The ignition was two loose wires clipped together by a clothespin. But it "ran like a top" on four patched and bulging tires. At least the price was right—$10.00 plus $2.50 for a new battery. Dalton painted the car red, white and blue.

A major summer event in the eastern part of the county was the all-day Fourth of July celebration in the Culpepper community just east of Readyville. Like similar programs in other area communities, the celebration featured

Dalton Stroop and cousin Charlotte Kerr in the '28 Chevy. *Photograph from the collection of Dalton Stroop.*

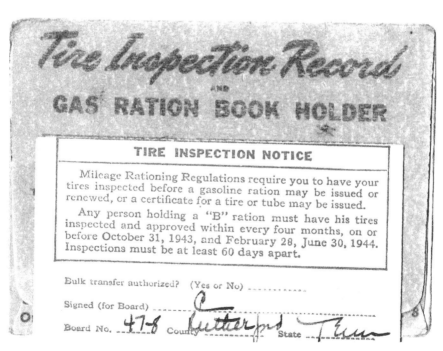

TIRE INSPECTION NOTICE

Mileage Rationing Regulations require you to have your tires inspected before a gasoline ration may be issued or renewed, or a certificate for a tire or tube may be issued.

Any person holding a "B" ration must have his tires inspected and approved within every four months, on or before October 31, 1943, and February 28, June 30, 1944. Inspections must be at least 60 days apart.

Bulk transfer authorized? (Yes or No) ....

Signed (for Board) ....

Board No. ..47-8.. County .... State ..Tenn..

Tire rationing.

lots of food, socializing, games for the kids and a rather serious baseball competition with prizes and bragging rights for area teams. The Culpepper event was held on the Readyville school grounds and was a community fundraiser for the school.

The 1941 event planners included a special competition with a five-dollar prize for the car that arrived carrying the most passengers. Dalton recruited riders from around the Halls Hill and Sharpsville communities, looking particularly for some smaller folks. His brother Robert, the Peay boys—Bill and Bob—and John Kerr were among the rider volunteers.

They loaded up the '28 Chevy with eighteen boys and young men and headed for Culpepper.

Despite the load, the old Chevy was making good progress until two tires blew out going up Bivens Hill. Dalton used a local farm telephone to call the Western Auto store on West Main in Murfreesboro. The store manager agreed to send a truck out with four new tires and to mount them on the spot for a total of five dollars per tire. Fifteen-year-old Robert Stroop remembers that twenty dollars was the most he had ever seen anyone, particularly his older brother, spend all at one time. Riding on their new "Davis Deluxe" tires, Dalton and his passengers made it to Culpepper and claimed the prize.

When Dalton returned to school for his senior year, the Chevy was used for the daily commute. On December 8, following the surprise attack on Pearl Harbor, the United States formally declared war and began the switch to a wartime economy. In January 1942, tires were the first item to be rationed because supplies of natural rubber were interrupted. A national speed limit of thirty-five miles per hour was soon adopted to conserve both fuel and tires. To receive a gasoline ration card, a person had to certify a need for gas and ownership of no more than five tires. All tires in excess of five per driver were subject to government confiscation. Also, rations could be denied to anyone owning tires not in use.

In the fall after graduation in 1942, Dalton went into the navy. The car was left behind, and the four relatively "new" tires were promptly sold for about double the original investment. (Auto tires continued to be unavailable throughout the war since all new production went to military needs. Rationing continued through the war, but as supplies of some items normalized, rationing was phased out. By the end of 1945, only sugar and rubber tires were still being rationed.)

In the meantime, younger brother Robert and several friends—all too young for the military—sought to put the Chevy back on the road using the original set of tires. "They were so full of holes that the inner tube would balloon out and burst," explains Robert. "So we tried packing them with sawdust. That was a failure, so we tried filling the old tires with concrete. That lasted for about a mile and then came all apart."

Finally, the boys parked the car in the garage, jacked up a rear wheel and placed a notched fireplace backlog under the elevated wheel. "We made a good walnut huller, after a few adjustments," remembers Stroop. "The nuts would come out like projectiles and crack when they hit the garage door, so we repositioned it farther from the door." After the nuts were hulled and dried, the boys sold them to Jim George, a nut and hides dealer at 308 Vine Street, Murfreesboro, for a penny a pound.

IV

PEOPLE

KADOSH FUNERAL FOR JAMES DANIEL RICHARDSON

"On a table near the coffin was a symbol of death wreathed with evergreens, surrounded by seven large candles, bearing no lights. At the head of the coffin stood a great iron passion cross, five feet in height." So reads one eyewitness account of the rare Knight Templar Kadosh funeral held at midnight in the Murfreesboro Central Christian Church on East Main in 1914.

Only two such funerals have ever been conducted in Tennessee. On this occasion, it was the last rites for Rutherford County native James Daniel Richardson, sovereign grand commander of the Supreme Council for the Southern Jurisdiction of the Scottish Rite Masons. (The Southern Jurisdiction includes thirty-five states and sixteen foreign countries.)

Richardson was born in Rutherford County in 1843, the son of John Watkins Richardson, a Murfreesboro physician and member of the Tennessee legislature. He served in the Confederate Tennessee 45th Infantry during the Civil War, attaining the rank of major.

While recovering from injuries as a prisoner of war in Alabama, he met and subsequently married Alabama R. Pippen. After the war, he entered law practice in Murfreesboro in partnership with General Joseph Palmer.

Following in his father's footsteps, he served in both the Tennessee House and Senate, serving as the youngest Speaker of the House from 1871 to 1873. He was elected to the U.S. Congress in 1884, representing the Fifth District, including Rutherford County, and served in the House for twenty years. While in Congress, he sponsored legislation that established the military park and national cemetery at the Stones River Battlefield. He also led the Democratic Party and chaired the 1904 Democratic National Convention.

Making his home at the corner of East Main and Academy in Murfreesboro, Richardson led the Rutherford County Fair Association, served as a director for two banks, was a commissioner for the Evergreen Cemetery and was a founder of the Central Christian Church. He also led fundraising for the Confederate monument that stands in the courthouse square. In response to a congressional resolution, Richardson compiled and edited *The Messages and Papers of the Presidents 1789–1897* and later prepared *The Messages and Papers of the Confederacy*, a compilation of the official records of the Confederate government.

As a thirty-third-degree Mason (inspector general) and sovereign commander, Richardson initiated construction of the House of the Temple, which serves as the headquarters of the Masonic Supreme Council in Washington, D.C. His Masonic leadership and other achievements are memorialized on a new Tennessee historical marker dedicated on September 14, 2008, at the corner where his home once stood. The corner at 302 East Main is now occupied by a former Kroger store building owned and used by the East Main Street Church of Christ. At one time, the Richardson home was used by the Jennings & Ayers Funeral Home, and the original front doors of the house are now part of the funeral home building on South Church Street.

The new marker is the result of research and application to the Tennessee Historical Commission by Jim Roberts, a great-grandson of the honoree. The $1,500 cost of the marker was shared by the great-grandchildren—Anne Byrn Roberts, Bradford Earl Roberts Jr., Virginia Byrn Sanders Huddleston, William Chase Ledbetter Jr., Sarah Byrn Evans Rickman, Susan Quarles Sanders and James Daniel Richardson ("Jim") Roberts.

For the midnight funeral service, one thousand curious onlookers saw the coffin hand-carried from the home to the church with a procession of 150 Masonic leaders from across the country in ceremonial dress. The eyewitness account of the private ceremony continues:

> *Nine candles four feet high stood in three triangles on the east, west and south side of the coffin. Each was lighted, but the chapel was otherwise dark. At the upper end of the coffin was laid a chaplet of white roses, and*

Seven great-grandchildren of Richardson gather around the new historical marker at the corner of Academy and East Main on Sunday, September 14, 2008. *Photograph courtesy of the Daily News Journal, Murfreesboro.*

---

below was the insignia of the order and the sword of the deceased Knight in its scabbard…The Preceptor preceded the body of officers…each bore lighted tapers and were attired in black with scarves of crepe. They entered the chapel singly, as silent as shadows. The Knights arranged themselves in a semicircle to the west, south and north sides of the coffin, all facing east. After a few moments of deathly silence, a trumpet sounded a plaintive note and the Master opened the ceremony.

The Master first asked for one who would accuse the dead, and when none appeared, the organ softly played Crossing the Bar. *The Expert and Sub-Expert then lifted the lid of the coffin and exposed the body of the dead Knight to view. His forehead was adorned with a chaplet of laurel and vine leaves. On his heart lay a freshly cut bunch of violets and on the breast a cross of gold set with sparkling jewels.*

The Knights then approached and each in turn touched the body with his right hand…accompanied with a blessing. The de profundis *was then chanted in Latin as the* libra nos *was chanted by the choir, their voices sounding farther and farther away. The coffin was then closed and taken aside while the choir sang mournful music…All tapers were extinguished*

except the Master's, and all the Knights kneeling...the Master struck the
iron cross three times and blessed the dead brother in ritual words.
On the morning of July 27, 1914, a public church service was conducted
by Reverend Everett S. Smith. At graveside in Evergreen Cemetery, services
were conducted by the local Masonic Order and the Confederate veterans.

The *Nashville Tennessean,* on July 28, 1914, reported on the funeral: "The altar of the church and the choir loft were completely hidden beneath the many floral offerings, representing the nation's grief over the loss of one of her noblest men."

"COMMODITIES BABY" BORN TO DETERMINED "HILL WOMAN"

On May 9, 1938, a young "hill woman" named Madie set out from her home in Sumner Hollow, near the Donnells Chapel community, to walk the twelve miles on Bradyville Pike to get "commodities" for her parents, Mollie and Ollie, and herself. Her father was not able-bodied, and the family depended largely on Madie to take in washing, tend the garden and generally support the family. She smoked a crooked stem pipe and was dressed in faded overalls, a ragged work shirt, a battered felt hat and a pair of men's work shoes; she was also unmarried and pregnant.

In the depths of the Great Depression, the Roosevelt administration implemented the "commodities program" to provide basic food items to families and individuals in need. This government largesse differed from the later food stamp program in that consumers had no discretion as to what food items they would receive. When potatoes were available, for example, every participant got potatoes. If you didn't get your distribution on the scheduled day, you had to wait until the next distribution.

The commodities program relied on some of the early farm support programs in which the federal government would buy directly from farmers at guaranteed prices. The distribution of commodities was discontinued in the early 1940s because of the shortages, rationing and full employment of the war period. In Rutherford County, the commodities were distributed by the Works Progress Administration office at the County Health Department.

As Madie came down out of the hills near the old Murray School, her time came. She gave birth to an eight-pound, blue-eyed baby boy in the girls' outhouse behind the school. She wrapped the newborn in newspaper and carefully placed it conspicuously in the fencerow near a school bus stop. Madie then continued her walk to town, where she picked up a peck of potatoes.

Carrying the potatoes, she hitched a ride part of the way home and walked the last few miles across the hills to her house. The next day, according to her own telling, she did a "family load" of washing for Clarence Denton, a neighboring farmer and store proprietor, cut the yard and worked the garden. Meanwhile, as Madie continued on her quest for commodities, a busload of schoolchildren had spotted the infant. "The bus had stopped and was about to go on when the girls by the left side windows started shouting, laughing and pointing,"

Madie Allen. *Photograph from the collection of Joe David Allen.*

remembers one who was on the bus. The baby was quickly provided care and admitted to the nursery at the Murfreesboro hospital, where it was determined to be in good health despite the exposure.

When maternity was determined, Madie was arrested, pending charges of abandoning and exposing her child. She was candid about the events and explained that she had left the child by the road hoping that someone would find it and care for it. Her circumstances, her sincere and understandable concern

Above: Madie and her "commodities baby" at age four.

Left: The "commodities baby" at age eight. *Both photographs from the collection of Joe David Allen.*

that her family get their allotment of commodities and her subsequent request "to have my baby back and go home" prompted sympathy, and Madie returned to Sumner Hollow with her son.

Local rumors and gossip as to the child's paternity held the attention of neighbors for some time. Early speculation focused on the school bus driver because of the child's roadside placement, but eventually the consensus settled on one of the more prominent and prosperous landowners in the community. Paternity, however, was never formally alleged or acknowledged. Some years later, in an incident unrelated to Madie and her child, the suspected father died in a shooting.

As for the child, Madie proved to be a capable mother, and her son is remembered as a well-behaved and bright student. "He grew up to be one of the best electricians in the county," observed Fred "Chigger" Wilson, a Murray School alumnus who remembers Madie and her "commodities baby."

THE "COMMODITIES BABY" (Joe David Allen) remembers that Madie, his mother, always carried a Barlow pocketknife. According to her own telling, she used the Barlow to cut the umbilical cord after the outhouse birth. Madie's own birth had been difficult; she was initially laid aside as a premature "stillborn" but survived to be a very strong and resolute woman. Neighbors remember seeing her running a wagon team while standing in the wagon and plowing rocky ground barefooted behind a mule.

Barbara Milligan remembers that in the late 1940s her father, Allen Barrett, pastor of Ward's Grove Baptist Church (1944–67), performed a private marriage service in the Barrett living room for Madie and a young man from the Halls Hill area while Madie's son waited outside in the car. Madie and her family lived on Trimble Road, and her son is remembered as a smart, quiet student at Kittrell. "He never was any trouble," recalls former Kittrell teacher Oma McNabb.

The "hill woman" characterization and physical description are taken directly from local news accounts published contemporary with the May 1938 events.

HOMELESS HOME BOY HOUSED UNDER POOL HALL

At the age of fifteen, Home Boy found himself back in his childhood community. His father was in Illinois with a second wife and believed that

Home Boy was in North Carolina with his mother. His mother knew that he had dropped out of school and run away. She assumed he had hitchhiked back to his father's home.

In fact, Home Boy was back in Rutherford County, where he and his parents had lived before the break-up. He was homeless. Looking for a place to "hang out," Home Boy found the Pastime Pool Hall to be an inviting environment and soon established himself as an open-to-close fixture.

The year was 1975, and the Pastime Pool Hall filled the area behind three storefronts on the west side of the courthouse square in Murfreesboro. Lovvorn's Watch Repair was in the center, and the pool hall wrapped around it. Today, the Pastime Barbershop occupies the old hall's north end, and the other end is now a retail shop. The square was still a principal business district for Murfreesboro, but the growth along Northwest Broad was having an effect on retailing; some people with foresight were already planning for the new interstate corridor. The activity in and around the Pastime reflected the current and changing community, as it had for many generations.

(An earlier generation will remember when the pool hall was on the south side of the square. The White Front Barbershop occupied one of the buildings on the west side between West Main and Vine Streets. The barbershop's name appropriately included the term "front" because it was indeed a front for a more lucrative enterprise—but that's another story.)

Desegregation of public facilities was still a new rule in 1975. The old Whites Only and Colored Section signs were gone from the Pastime, but Home Boy recalls a general understanding that one end of the room was for black players, and the rest was for whites only. "But in fact," remembers Home Boy, "everybody played with anybody at whichever table was open. Your status was determined by your skill and your willingness to wager."

Home Boy quickly befriended the Pastime operator, Norris Lovvorn, and was soon running errands, sweeping and emptying trash for a few dollars a day. But at closing time, Home Boy was still homeless. This he remedied, unbeknownst to the property owners, by breaking into the basement off the alley and creating a private living space under the pool hall. "It was a dugout basement with a concrete floor. I spliced into the pool hall wiring and plugged in a light and an old refrigerator," he now confesses. "I tapped into the water line and had running water that drained out into the alley. I drug in an old mattress to sleep on."

As his skill with a pool cue improved, Home Boy began hustling for extra income. He also was becoming quite handy with tools as the "fix-it" guy for the pool hall.

Home Boy. *Photograph by Greg Tucker.*

One day on the street, Home Boy was surprised to encounter his father, who was again single and had recently returned to the area. The reunion was good for both father and son, and Home Boy abandoned his secret lodgings to live again with his dad. His daytime routine continued at the pool hall, but he found it increasingly difficult to find a "mark" who would play him for money.

At least his father knew where to find him and would regularly call the pool hall and ask Lovvorn to send his son home. Lovvorn would turn from the phone and shout, "Home, boy!" The name stuck.

After a hitch in the army and a series of jobs in North Carolina, Georgia, Tennessee and Florida as a truck driver, tree trimmer, plumber, carpenter, rough-in electrician, roofer, gambler and plant worker, David "Home Boy" Kline settled back in Rutherford County and now runs a successful handyman service. He still gets out his custom pool cue on occasion. In his last tournament, he placed third behind world-ranked women's champion Connie Lee and Johnny Archer. (Archer performed the pool cue action for Paul Newman and Tom Cruise in the movie *The Color of Money.*)

UNDERWATER RECOVERY PIONEER

SCUBA Recovery at Murfree Spring

While anchored off the Isle of Crete in the Mediterranean Sea in 1958, U.S. Navy seaman Jim Haynes from Rutherford County saw his first Aqua Lung.

"A fellow came on board to demonstrate this new equipment for swimming and breathing underwater without hoses and ropes," remembers Haynes. "After some brief instruction, I tried it and liked it, so I bought one of his outfits."

This self-contained diving device, originally called the Aqua-Lung, was developed in 1942 by two Frenchmen, Jacques-Yves Cousteau and Emile Gagnon. It consisted of a face mask and mouthpiece with a hose connected to a tank of compressed air worn on the diver's back. The key feature was a "regulator," which responded to the user's breathing reflex. Over the next decade, the diving device was used and further developed by the military and professional divers. Subsequently dubbed SCUBA (an acronym for "self-contained underwater breathing apparatus"), sport diving was popularized by Lloyd Bridges on *Sea Hunt* and other film and television exposure. But the equipment for recreational and sport diving was not generally available until the mid-1960s.

Back home in Murfreesboro in 1959, Haynes and his buddy, Bobby Jernigan, went almost every weekend to Center Hill Lake for diving and spear-fishing. "My mother certainly did not trust this strange equipment, and probably doubted my judgment," says Haynes, "but we survived and developed a lot of confidence and underwater experience."

There were no certified trainers or dive shops in the area during this period, and the only place to refill tanks with filtered air was in Nashville for one dollar per tank. Eventually, Haynes was able to purchase a number of aviation air tanks and modify them for diving. He also rigged up his own compressor and filtering equipment to fill the tanks. Although filling a tank took several hours, it was still quicker and cheaper than going to Nashville.

Haynes kept his diving equipment at his workplace— Lakeland Marine, Inc., at 121 Northwest Broad. This in-town proximity was in part why he became involved in his first underwater recovery. On a warm, sunny spring day in March 1964, a neighborhood boy plunged into the natural pool behind the icehouse/bottling plant on Broad and never resurfaced, apparently overcome by the unexpectedly cold water. Police and fire personnel

Boy Drowns In Cold Pool

MURFREESBORO — A 12-year-old boy drowned yesterday when he apparently suffered cramps after diving into a pool of water fed by an underground spring, Police Chief William Chambliss said.

Dead is Freddie Smith, son of Mrs. Annie Smith Crockett of Murfreesboro.

Chambliss said the youth went to the pool with two other boys, stripped off his clothing and dived into the cold water while the others waited on the bank.

The boys said Smith "came up two or three times and sank," Chambliss said.

An hour later, Jim Haynes, a skindiver, recovered the body lodged under a rock ledge, about 15 feet below the surface, the chief said.

The pool is located near the city water filtration plant.

Jim Haynes prepares to dive in the deep pool below the Murfree Spring. Murfreesboro police chief William Chambliss holds down a ladder during the search for a missing child. *Photograph from the Jim Haynes collection.*

knew that Haynes was a diver with equipment nearby, so they asked for his help in recovering the child's body.

By the time Haynes got on the scene with his equipment, word had spread, and a large neighborhood crowd had gathered in the area below Murfree Spring. The pool was actually a sinkhole that overflowed to Town Creek. The water also flowed under a bluff into the underground. A long ladder was placed in the pool so the diver would not have to "free dive" in the dark water. "As I began the search, I was concerned that the body may have disappeared into the sink beyond recovery," recounts Haynes.

There was no visibility in the murky water, so Haynes had to feel his way.

"I had about decided to give up the search when my hand touched a foot that was hung on a branch. I figure the branch kept the body from being swept out of reach under the bluff," explains Haynes. "This was my first experience with a drowning victim, and I was pretty shook up by the contact."

Regaining his composure, Haynes worked the foot loose from the branches, and swam to the surface, where a waiting policeman grabbed the foot and called for some of the onlookers to form a human chain to pass the body up the bluff to a waiting ambulance. "The neighborhood crowd scattered at the sight of the body," remembers Haynes. "We finally got enough fire and police personnel involved to get the body up to the roadway."

The site of the tragic drowning and first scuba-aided recovery in Murfreesboro is today part of the water gardens behind the Children's Discovery Center. The cave spring, natural pool and sink have been substantially filled in and altered. The steep bluff has been partially lowered by parking-area paving. The end of a garden walkway overlooks where the ladder was placed for the diver's initial descent.

Haunting Search Was Final Recovery

Jim Haynes was the only person in Rutherford County whom fire and police personnel knew to be experienced in underwater search and recovery in the early 1960s. In or about the summer of 1965, a Sewart Air Force Base airman decided to try the rope swing hanging from a tree above the dam at the old Walter Hill powerhouse. He swung out, plunged in and never surfaced.

The sheriff's department asked Haynes to assist in recovering the body. He arrived on the scene at about 4:00 p.m. Hours had elapsed since the

Walter Hill Dam and powerhouse, January 2010. *Photograph by Greg Tucker.*

disappearance of the swimmer, and the military had already contacted the airman's family. The parents arrived on-site in the late afternoon.

On this occasion, Haynes brought a dozen small air tanks. He had earlier purchased the tanks at a surplus sale at Sewart. They were originally used by pilots for in-flight oxygen at high altitudes. Haynes refitted the tanks with "J-valves" for underwater use. He had a local seamstress custom make a diving vest with a back pouch so he could quickly and easily pull and replace an empty tank. To avoid the time and expense of taking the tanks to Nashville to be filled, Haynes had rigged a small compressor and filter so he could fill the tanks in his shop.

The water was "pretty chilly," and visibility in the water was near zero. Using a small underwater light, Haynes still could see only a few inches. He used a knotted rope to pattern his search. Recalling events of forty-five years earlier, Haynes remembers appreciatively that Floyd Lamb, owner of Lamb's Restaurant & Motel on Lebanon Pike, kept rescue personnel supplied with sandwiches and hot coffee.

After about four hours of searching, exhausting most of his air supply with daylight fading, Haynes advised those on the scene that he would have to stop for the day and resume the search in the morning. The mother of the missing airman pleaded for the search to continue, and Haynes agreed to make one more sweep across the area.

"I went down and began following my rope, crawling along on my stomach, feeling ahead with one hand and holding my light with the other. My face was just above the bottom with about six inches of visibility," remembers Haynes. Suddenly, Haynes came face to face with the body, which was lying face-up on the bottom—mouth and eyes wide open. "It more than startled me, and for years that face would replay in my thoughts and nightmares," recalls Haynes. Grabbing the shirt, Haynes surfaced, and ambulance personnel quickly took over handling the body. A few days later, Haynes advised local officials that he would no longer be available for recovery work.

Almost a decade later, area rescue squads were relying on another volunteer, Buddy Towery, for scuba search and recovery. Like Haynes, Towery, owner of a garage and wrecker service, used his own equipment and paid his own expenses. He worked with the county sheriff and with Lavergne, Smyrna and Rutherford County volunteer rescue units. In the mid- to late 1970s, prompted in part by the high level of recreational activity on the relatively new Percy Priest Lake, Mike Nunnelly, now the head of the Rutherford County Ambulance and Rescue Service, helped organize and instruct a continuing education course in "public safety diving" at Middle Tennessee State University (MTSU). Ron Nelson led the instruction, and he and Nunnelly "wrote the book" for this first-of-its-kind training program. Fifteen local rescue volunteers completed the course. A decade later, however, only two volunteer divers were still assisting the local rescue units—Jack Kiesling and John Hettish.

"Public safety diving takes its toll—physically and emotionally—especially on volunteers," explains Nunnelly, who has himself been diving since he was fifteen. In 1992, on Nunnelly's initiative, ten county ambulance service and sheriff's department personnel took professional dive rescue instruction in Colorado, and the county invested in the appropriate equipment. Today, the ambulance service includes a team of well-equipped professional rescue personnel with dive training and experience. Chris Clark is the team leader.

Retired Dairy Farmer Older than
Local Johnson Grass

Ed Jordan. *Photograph by Greg Tucker.*

Ed Jordan is old enough to remember when there was no Johnson grass in Rutherford County and when there was at least one itinerant rock crusher making calls around the county. Jordan, retired dairy farmer and former chairman of the county school board, turned eighty-two in September 2009.

Johnson grass has been in Rutherford County about as long as Jordan. He remembers that the local farm on which he was raised had no Johnson grass as late as 1938, but it was coming. The grass is known today as a "pernicious weed" and an invasive exotic that crowds out desirable forage and cash crops. The weed can cause "bloat" in herbivores and may contain sufficient amounts of prussic acid to kill cattle and horses when wilted from frost or drought. A perennial grass spreading both by seed and underground stems, it can be controlled only by herbicides and continuous mowing.

But in the early twentieth century, it was promoted as the original "wonder grass" that could replace most other forage crops because of its rapid growth, size and hardiness. A native of the Mediterranean perimeter, Johnson grass (*Sorghum halepense*) is believed to be the original cultivated sorghum of the Ancient World.

"Sometime around 1930, a fellow named Miller saw an ad for this new 'wonder grass' in a magazine and decided to try it," recalls Jordan. "He had a farm on the Manchester Pike (on the left going away from Murfreesboro in what is now about the 1500 block) where he planted the mail-order seed. He hay-baled the Johnson grass and sold it all over the county." The "wonder grass" quickly spread to neighboring farms along Manchester Pike and eventually spread by hay distribution and other means across the county. Jordan remembers that during this period people used to see James M. Haynes, first president of the Rutherford County Farm Bureau, out with a "grubbing hoe and gunny sack" digging up the Johnson grass in a single-handed, and singularly unsuccessful, effort to stop the spread. (Haynes served as bureau president from 1923 to 1927. His farm was on the Lebanon Pike and included the land now occupied by the new post office.)

But Johnson grass is not the only exotic introduced in Rutherford County by a Manchester Pike farmer. In 1949, Ramsey Snell read about bird's-foot trefoil clover in a farm publication. After consulting with soil conservationist Don Anderson, he ordered seed and planted ten acres. Three years later, he had twenty acres planted in the new clover (now called Japanese clover by some locals) and was hosting visitors from around the mid-state who were considering the new forage crop. The clover was promoted around the area as a "long-lived perennial legume" having "high palatability and nutritive value" and thriving in clay loam soils. "There has never been a known case of bloat on trefoil," claimed some advocates.

Today, however, the yellow-flowered clover persists primarily in permanent pasture mixed with other grasses and legumes. "Occasionally a troublesome weed," according to some sources, bird's-foot trefoil is now a relatively inconspicuous pasture volunteer contributing modestly to the diets of local grazing stock. By comparison to Johnson grass, that's a pretty good result for an exotic forage crop first grown in Rutherford County on a Manchester Pike farm.

So what is an "itinerant rock crusher"? Jordan explains that farmers needed lime for their alfalfa crop, and in the 1930s agricultural lime in Rutherford County was basically home grown. "We would pile brick-sized rock out by the road and once a year in the fall the rock crusher would come to the farm and crush up our pile of rocks," remembers Jordan. The crusher rolled on steel wheels pulled by a tractor. Once in place by the farmer's rock pile, the crusher was run by belt off the tractor. The rocks were hand fed into a hopper, and the crushed limestone was dumped out in a pile. "We then had to shovel the lime into a wagon, which was pulled into the field where we shoveled and spread it for the alfalfa crop." Jordan thinks the crusher operator charged a dollar a ton but admits that the finances "weren't any of my concern" at that time.

Sam Woods, DVM, cared for animals in Rutherford County from 1944 to 1981. Regarding Johnson grass poisoning, he remembers when Dick Martindale brought fifteen cows from Indiana to his farm on Manson Pike. When they were unloaded, they were apparently hungry after the ride and began grazing. The whole load developed Johnson grass poisoning. "I had five IVs going at one time. I think they all recovered," recalls Woods.

The doctor does not remember ever seeing a horse with Johnson grass poisoning, but cattle problems were common. "The old wives' tale that the grass is poison only at certain stages is not so, for I have seen it kill a cow when the grass is two inches high and when it is a head high."

Myers Parsons, a retired businessman and former high school agricultural sciences teacher, believes that the farmers got little benefit from the rock crushing. "The lime needs to be a fine, soluble powder for the plant to absorb," says Parsons. "The coarse gravel from the old rock crusher did little good for the alfalfa."

For Jordan's eighty-third birthday, however, forage crops were not considered. Instead, his sons, Will and Buddy, gave their father a new bright red Chevrolet Silverado 4x4 pickup truck. Jordan figures the birthday truck cost him about eighty dollars. "My old truck disappeared for a trade-in just after I filled the gas tank," he said.

"BISCUIT TEA" MIRACLE SAVED LIFE OF RUTHERFORD CHILD

Be not forgetful to entertain strangers; for thereby some have entertained angels unaware.
—Hebrews 13:2

Mort Sweeney was determined to have his own place before he married Maude. Finally, in 1910, near his thirtieth birthday, he made a deal for a small farm off Couchville Pike with a spring branch that flowed south to the Stones River in the remote northern tip of Rutherford County. Anxious to start their family and make a home, Maude was soon expecting, and Mort worked steadily to make their farm productive. When her time came, Maude suffered a difficult birth. The child lived only a few days, and the midwife called it "stone death" because the infant appeared to become rigid before it ceased breathing.

They buried their firstborn near the house, confirmed their faith in a loving and just Lord and continued on. A year later, the farm was beginning to yield a return on their hard work, the house had a picketed front yard with a few carefully tended rose bushes and Maude was again with child. This time, they were blessed with a beautiful, healthy daughter they named Bob Marie.

Soon after the birth, Maude brought the infant to her breast and was pleased by the hungry way the child enjoyed her first meal and eventually slipped into a contented nap. But within an hour, the child awakened, spitting up all that she had consumed. Subsequent feedings

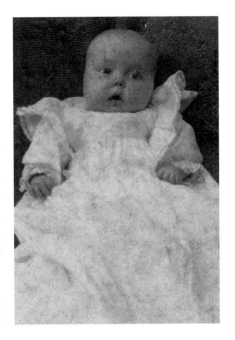

Vesta Sweeney, Mort's first daughter.
Photograph from the collection of Bob Marie Sweeney Freeman.

had the same result, and by the third day it was evident that the infant was waning. The midwife, neighbors and family offered advice and sympathy. Maude tried cow's milk, and a neighbor brought goat's milk, but the result was the same. By the third day, Bob Marie was pale, thin and lethargic. Soon, it became apparent that the child would not survive.

Mort suffered and grieved over his own helplessness as the child wasted and Maude sank deeper into hopeless despair. At daybreak, he hitched the mules and drove them to the field. Maude positioned the cradle just inside the open door. The only response from the starving child was a quiver of movement and a labored breath. Maude stepped out on the porch, and with head bowed and hands cupped over her mouth and nose, she prayed for the soul of her dying child. At about that same moment, Mort reached the field and stopped to adjust the harnesses. Overcome by emotion, he leaned his head against the neck of the mule and prayed silently for his child and wife.

Maude's prayer was interrupted by the sound of the picket gate. She looked up to see an elderly stranger walking across the small yard. The woman wore a shawl, and her plain skirt almost brushed the ground as she walked. Without greeting or introduction, she said, "I hear you have a sick child. You must give her biscuit tea." As Maude stood with hands still clasped, the old woman explained how to prepare the tea. She ended by saying, "Feed it to the child from a silver spoon."

Without a word, Maude turned and dashed to the old family press next to the stove. There she found several dry biscuits left from the previous day. With trembling hand, she crushed the biscuits in a bowl, poured boiling water over them and then stirred and mashed them into a watery gruel. When the mixture cooled, she poured it through a fine sieve into a mug. Finding a small, loop-handled spoon that had been her own as a child, she cradled Bob Marie upright in her arm and gently forced the spoon between the child's tiny lips. With a second spoonful, she saw the child swallow. After administering less than a quarter of a cup in this manner, she lay the now sleeping infant in her crib. An hour later, the child stirred, and Maude repeated the feeding. This continued through the day.

As the workday ended, Mort headed for the house expecting the worst—a dead child and a grieving mother. As he walked heavily from the barn, Maude suddenly ran through the doorway into his arms, tears flowing, and shouted, "She's getting better!" At first he thought his wife was hysterical, but she pulled him into the house, where the child's appearance convinced him that a miracle had indeed occurred. The tale was quickly told of the woman stranger and biscuit tea. They sat through the night watching and feeding little Bob Marie and giving prayerful thanks that their child's life had been spared.

Mort and Maude Sweeney with Bob Marie as a healthy toddler. *Photograph from the collection of Bob Marie Sweeney Freeman.*

Word spread through the community as neighbors came to offer sympathy and found joyous, rather than grieving, parents. But no one could identify the stranger whose advice had apparently saved the child. When Mort later inquired at the Cotton Hill crossroads, none could recall any such person on that day or any time before or since.

(A generation after Mort and Maude, medical science began to understand milk allergies, one of the most common food allergies in children. Gastrointestinal hypersensitivity causes nausea and vomiting with a quick, acute onset. Maude's biscuit recipe contained a lot of nourishing animal fat and protein: flour, baking powder, salt, lard and sour milk or buttermilk. The baking and other ingredients apparently change the chemical structure of the milk allergen.)

Bob Marie grew to be an active tomboy. She eventually married and raised a daughter. As Mort and Maude aged, she brought them into her home and tended them until they passed on. She died at the age of eighty-six.

This family history was originally documented by Anita S. Tucker, first cousin of Bob Marie and mother of Greg Tucker.

ROCKVALE'S DOC: SCHOOLS, SPORTS, SHOES AND SERVICE

Like most folks in his generation, Thomas Poplin Burns came into this world at home in 1901 with the country doctor's horse and buggy waiting in the yard. He was the last of ten siblings and half siblings and was named for the doctor who delivered him—Thomas I. Poplin, MD, from Midland. Naturally, the nickname "Doc" soon followed. He apparently took to it, for on any introduction he would say, "My name is Doc."

Doc enjoyed life, centered on the Rockvale community and the many people who filled it. Longtime friend Bubba Woodfin said, "Everything about Doc was friendly...and funny." The late Elmer Hinton, a Nashville newspaper columnist and Rockvale fan, once wrote, "Doc is the type who never runs out of funny things to say or pranks to pull...just to be around him you'd think he never had...a serious thought in his life...his favorite stories were usually about himself."

Recounting a trip through Mississippi with a companion, Doc told of a teenager they encountered. Doc addressed him with a friendly "Howdy, young man!" The young fellow, apparently not having a good day, responded

Thomas I. Poplin, MD, from Midland with his horse Almont. Small saddlebags carried medical equipment and supplies. *Photograph from the Tucker family collection.*

Card night at the Rockvale garage. Doc Burns is at the far right. *Photograph from the collection of Sarah Burns Frizzell.*

with a sharp and profane comment on Doc's character and lineage. As the teenager walked away, Doc's companion queried, "How'd he know about you away down here?"

Doc got eight years of formal education and then went to work wherever he could get hired. In 1922, he married Vera Looney, whose family had a prosperous farm off Swamp Road near Eagleville. Farmer Looney, concerned that Doc's income was a bit uncertain, provided housing and a steady job farming. After several months of daylight-to-dark labor, the rain came pouring down one morning and appeared to have set in for the day.

Mr. and Mrs. J.P. "Doc" Burns.

Expecting a long-overdue day off, Doc spent the day in the barn shucking corn with his daddy-in-law and bagging the shucks for pig feed. It was then that he realized that his true ambition and future was in retailing—he would be a storekeeper. Soon he had a partner and took over the store in Concord. Doc was a fair and friendly storekeeper, and folks liked him. His motto (on a sign by the cash register) was: "We can't please everybody, but we try!" The store prospered, and eventually Doc had interests in other stores in Rockvale and Salem. He also began generously giving back to his community.

"Doc." *Both photographs from the collection of Sarah Burns Frizzell.*

117

Thomas P. "Doc" Burns as a young man. *Photograph from the collection of Sarah Burns Frizzell.*

The Rockvale garage. *Photograph from the collection of Sarah Burns Frizzell.*

"Whenever anyone was in trouble, or sick, or if there was a death in the family, Daddy was always there," remembers daughter Sarah Frizzell. "I remember when we were children, how often we sat and waited in the car outside someone's home while Daddy and Mama did what they could for the family…Daddy always felt sorry for those without transportation and would pick up anyone walking and take them wherever, sober or not."

When the father of a large family died, Doc organized the men of the community to tend to the family's large cotton crop. When Bud Carlton got very sick, Doc got a group of neighbors to bring in the crop. Doc even maintained one of the local cemeteries, pouring concrete and stenciling replacement headstones. During the Depression, Doc extended credit to anyone in need—which was most everybody—and had to go back to farming for a while as a result.

While working at the store, Doc usually had some prank in the planning or in play. The store was on a party-line telephone, and Doc enjoyed "exposing" those who were listening in. He would ring his own number and say, for example, "I'm sorry to hear he died!" Then he would quickly hang up and wait to see who would call the store and inquire as to who died. "He caught his own sister that way," remembered the late Willie Floyd Williams.

"Doc sold shoes but would keep the shoebox and put it back on the shelf whenever he sold a pair," recalled Williams. "For a small country store, it looked like he carried a really big stock of shoes. When the shoe factory reps came by, they were always impressed." According to Doc, that's why one of the companies offered to put him on the road as a salesman. He took the job.

Doc was a hardcore sports fan. Whenever a Rockvale school team played, he was in the stands, and everyone knew he was there. Part of the enjoyment of the game for Doc was aggravating the other side and harassing the officials—all in good fun, unless the opponent was archrival Eagleville. "Doc thought some of the Eagleville fans were not only as loud as himself but also kind of abusive." Williams remembered that Doc went over to the opposition side of the gym to say a few words about "good sportsmanship" but ended up missing the rest of the game "to get his tongue stitched up."

Doc was not only a fan but also an active sportsman. "Probably one of the best croquet players in Rockvale," suggested Williams. When the grass court next to the school was paved over, Doc built a "professional" packed sand court next to his store. "Played like cement," Williams recalled. "Most of us preferred grass." Doc even got himself a competition-style mallet, "one of those short-handled jobs."

Doc and his son-in-law, Ken Frizzell, entered a state doubles tournament in Nashville. In the first round, they were matched against a team from Lafayette. Doc was confident: "I've been to Lafayette, and there ain't a place there level 'nuff to play on." Frizzell notes that the Rockvale team went home early.

Fishing was a life-long passion and fit well with Doc's tenure as an itinerant shoe salesman. He never went on the road without his tackle. If he heard they were hitting "below the boils" at Pickwick, he knew it was time to make a few sales calls down in Hardin County.

In his sixties, Doc took up golf, playing often and enthusiastically. He would boast of "shooting his age…on the front nine!" When his eyesight got so bad he couldn't see the flag or the hole, Bealer Smotherman used slats from window blinds to fashion large arrows. Doc's playing partners would lay the arrows by his ball to line up his shot. "Doc loved the game for as long as he was able to play," remembered one of his neighbors. "He even put on short britches!"

In 1944, Doc was elected to the Rutherford County Board of Education. He served for twenty-one years, including five years as chairman without ever campaigning or soliciting a vote.

Note: Greg Tucker caddied and kept score for Doc Burns and two of his regular golf buddies—M.B. Brandon and Burney Tucker.

Great Big Fellow Liked Kids, Not Doctors

Ira Jackson "Dutch" Allen was "a great big fellow," remembers Thomas Cooper, one of his ten stepchildren. As a child, he spoke with a slight impediment. One of the "loafers" at the general store heard him and said, "Boy, you talk like a Dutchman!" The name suited him.

Short on formal education, Dutch relied mainly on his size and incomparable strength to make his way. He tenant farmed all over the southeast section of Rutherford County and did whatever "day work" was available. "I doubt there was a family in the district that he hadn't done some work for during the 1930–50 period," noted Cooper. The only "regular" job he had was as the custodian for the Murray School for several

Dutch Allen. *Photograph from the collection of Joe David Allen.*

years, but when school money got tight he was laid off. "Some of the school kids took over lighting the fire and cleaning up," recalls Joe Allen, a nephew of Dutch.

Cooper recalls that about a year after his father died in 1934, his mother, Lillie Mai Cooper, moved to Murfreesboro to take a job "making bib overalls." The work was part of the "back to work" effort of the Roosevelt administration. "Some company in town got a contract to make overalls," explained Cooper. "She was paid about seventeen dollars for twenty hours of work."

Widow Cooper and her five children lived in the Westvue neighborhood in a house rented from Guy James Sr. for two dollars a week. (The running water was a community spigot at the end of the street. The toilet was conveniently behind the house.) They got by, in part, because Dutch would come by regularly bringing produce from the country. "I was about eight

121

years old when I watched him use a potato fork to turn up a big garden for us," recalls Cooper. "He was about the same age as my oldest sister, Leonnie, but he got along real good with all of us and helped us a lot."

Folks along Bradyville Pike figured Dutch was courtin' one of the Cooper girls, but he surprised his neighbors when he announced his plan to marry Lillie Mai. According to nephew Allen, when somebody asked Dutch why he proposed to the mother (twenty years his senior) instead of one of the daughters, Dutch said, "This way I get 'em all!"

When the town work ran out, Dutch moved his family out to Rock Hill, where he tenant farmed and took up timbering. "I once watched him cut off a foot-thick log with an old, nubbed axe," recalls Allen. "It took him four licks!"

Dutch had no use for doctors or hospitals. When the church bus rolled over and everybody aboard was banged up pretty bad, Dutch crawled out and walked home. Once, while cutting timber, the axe glanced off and hit him in the leg. He finished the workday and walked home with a bandana tied around the wound. That night, Lillie Mai saw blood leaking from his boot and discovered that he was still bleeding from a deep cut. Only threats from his landlord, A.J. Todd, persuaded Dutch to see a doctor. "They had to put on a tourniquet to stop the bleeding where he had cut an artery," recounts Cooper.

When a tree fell and broke his leg, Dutch hobbled home and waited three days before getting it set. "He insisted on a cast that he could walk on so he wouldn't miss any work." Through it all, Dutch provided for his family. "He worked hard, and he was a good dad."

With all of her children grown and independent, Lillie Mai died in 1966. Dutch saw to her burial next to her first husband, Joe Cooper. Several years later, Dutch was again courtin' a financially strapped, single mother with five children, now some twenty years his junior. "I like kids," explained the big fellow.

Despite being advised against the marriage by Pastor Kittrell Lowe, Dutch wed again and moved his new bride, Allie, and her children into his Rock Hill home. Soon, there were rumors in the neighborhood about Allie's temperament.

By the mid-1970s, the Great Society subsidy programs were in place, and both Dutch and his wife were receiving monthly entitlement checks. The two checks were usually delivered on the same day, and Dutch would walk to the Sewell Summers store in Donnells Chapel to cash them. He always gave Allie her cash and kept his own.

On February 3, 1976, only the monthly check for Dutch was delivered by the rural mail carrier. Dutch walked to the store with one of the children, got his cash, bought some candy for the child and returned home, where Allie confronted him. She demanded her money and didn't believe his explanation.

In a fit of anger, Allie pointed a .22-caliber pistol at Dutch and threatened to shoot if her money was not immediately delivered. Dutch turned his back and walked into the bedroom, closing the door behind him. Allie fired once through the closed door, and the bullet struck her husband in the back just above the waist.

The next day, a neighbor reported to Sheriff Robert Goodwin that Dutch Allen was dead. When the coroner arrived, he found Dutch "clean and serene" in his bed. Allie gave her description of events, and the death was officially ruled a "massive coronary."

Despite Allie's insistence that the body be buried without the expense of a commercial mortuary, other family members called Woodfin Funeral Chapel to remove and prepare the body. Woodfin personnel found a band-aid covering a small hole in the back and sent the body to the hospital for analysis. An autopsy determined that Dutch had bled to death from internal injuries resulting from a small-caliber slug penetrating a kidney and other vital organs.

Allie was arrested and charged with homicide. The full story was told by an eyewitness, one of her daughters, who had been forced to help with the cover-up, even putting pictures on the door to hide the bullet hole. Before trial, Allie was found to be incompetent and institutionalized. After a relatively short stay in the criminal asylum, she was released to the custody of a family member. "She wasn't crazy," observed a neighbor, "just mean!"

GREEN MONEY WAS GOOD IF IT LOOKED GOOD

When President Abraham Lincoln signed the Legal Tender Act in 1862 (authorizing the first American use of paper money), he funded the Civil War with paper backed by only the "full faith and credit" of the U.S. government. He also created a bonanza for counterfeiters.

According to Lynn Glaser, author of *Counterfeiting in America* (1960), in the years during and shortly after the war, about half the paper currency in circulation in the country was counterfeit. In the former Confederate states, the percentage was even higher, but few cared. Compared to the abundant and worthless Confederate money, and the notes issued by local banks, "green money" was good, if it looked good, regardless.

In Rutherford County, a shrewd and successful entrepreneur named Reuben Christian Harrell had smartly bet against the "home team" by accepting and holding only U.S. "greenbacks." He avoided being a combatant, and with cash on hand, he spent the war years rounding up horses and mules (and anything else abandoned by the various military units) and selling to whomever had greenbacks to spend.

Not trusting either the soundness or integrity of commercial banks, he was nevertheless known to local bankers. When he had a quantity of small bills, he would go to a local bank and exchange for larger denominations. (Fives, tens and twenties were the most popular denominations for the counterfeiters of the era.) His dealings and business success earned him the nickname "Greenback Rube," and during the Reconstruction years he was one of the few locals with ready cash.

Born in the 1820s and raised "dirt poor" in a remote part of the county, Greenback had no formal education and no inherited assets. When he first married, he and his wife settled in a one-room cabin in the southeast Rutherford hills. Their bed was a mound of straw.

To support his early farming efforts, he attempted to buy a relatively trivial amount of goods on credit from the local store, but his credit request was refused. Greenback vowed then that he would never again attempt a purchase without cash in hand. He hung a pair of worn overalls on a nail in his house, tied knots in the pants legs and dropped every penny he earned into the overalls.

According to a Harrell family history: "Making do with the bare minimum of necessities while scratching out every dollar he could earn," Greenback had by the prewar years accumulated enough cash to "buy land and property shrewdly with a keen eye" to current and future values. When he found a good buy, he offered cash on the spot and immediately went to the courthouse to record the deed.

As a result of his land transactions and a substantial farming operation, he was positioned to benefit from business opportunities that arose during the war and Reconstruction years for someone with ready cash. He was said to be "tight as the bark on a tree, but anything he said he would do, he did…and he would always help a neighbor who really needed help." Ike Wade, an elderly descendant of freed slaves who lived near Depot Hill until the 1950s, remembered Greenback: "He was a hard man to work for or to trade with, but he was as honest as the day is long."

On one occasion several years after the war, Greenback offered his cotton crop to a local ginner and cotton broker. When Greenback complained about the low price offered, the broker explained that he already had a large cotton inventory in the warehouse. Greenback bought everything in the warehouse for a price slightly higher than he had been offered and paid cash. Several months later, he cleared the inventory and made an impressive profit.

Greenback also took care of his family. Despite his success with little or no schooling, he encouraged all of his children to complete their schooling and provided the funding as needed. Several attended college and entered various professions.

When his son, Thomas Harrell, got in some serious trouble and wound up in the county jail, neighbors were told that Thomas had died of some mysterious ailment while locked up. Greenback personally claimed the body in a sealed casket that was not opened for any purpose prior to burial. It was later rumored that Greenback had bought Thomas' release and financed his relocation out West.

By the time of his death in the 1890s, Greenback had extensive holdings along Bradyville Pike as far out as Donnells Chapel. His will gave equal

The architecturally unique Harrell/Todd farmhouse at 2523 Bradyville Pike was demolished in 2009 for construction of a new church facility. The Italianate style of the porch and entry evidenced a family of means in the late nineteenth century. *Photograph by Greg Tucker.*

Greenback's crypt in a remote family cemetery off Bradyville Pike. *Photograph by Kevin G. Tucker.*

value to each of his six surviving children (with Thomas's share going to the respective grandchildren). Reflecting his aversion to debt, his will specified that the bequests would not be distributed until seven years after his death and then only to those who were free of debt.

Greenback's son, John Wesley Harrell, lived on his inheritance, a farm about three miles from Murfreesboro (now on the edge of the Murfreesboro city limits at 2523 Bradyville Pike). Victoria Harrell, daughter of John Wesley Harrell, married W.T. Todd from Coffee County in 1898, and recent generations have called the farm "the Todd Place." The Harrell/Todd home was demolished in 2009, and the Grace Baptist Church is now planned for what remains of the property.

As Greenback lay dying, he discussed the hereafter with his attending physician, Dr. James Madison Dill (for whom Dilton is named). Greenback observed that his numerous farms and properties had many gates and roads, and he knew where they all led, but he did not know what was beyond the gate now before him.

GAMBLING COLLATERAL BECAME SMYRNA LANDMARK

Gilbert Olerud was raised in his family's general store in Fargo, North Dakota. He learned firsthand that commercial success comes from being part of the community. He knew nothing about gambling collateral, but his Tennessee venture became a landmark and a significant part of the commercial and social history of a Rutherford community.

Gamblers' collateral in the 1940s, this store on Jefferson Pike developed into Gilsville, a landmark in the Smyrna community. *Photograph from the Olerud family collection.*

Fresh out of high school and married to Mavis Nilsson, his childhood sweetheart, Olerud joined the U.S. Air Force and served in World War II and Korea before being posted to Sewart Air Force Base in 1952. Anticipating his discharge while living off base in a local trailer court, Olerud appreciated the virtues of Smyrna and saw his future in a small corner store and trailer park for sale a few blocks east of the air base.

Gambill's Grocery & Trailer Court was owned by Vincent Gambill and was for sale in 1953, business and property, for $4,000. The store was a simple frame structure wrapped in brick-patterned tarpaper with a Gulf sign and two pumps. A large Royal Crown Cola sign above the porch and a Double Cola sign nailed to a tree promised a variety of consumer choices. Although he was raised under a Coca-Cola sign with Phillips 66 pumps in North Dakota, Olerud bought the Smyrna business and property.

According to Smyrna lore, the store property was part of a larger transfer of property from James D. Hale to Gambill to satisfy a gambling debt. Unfortunately, county deed records do not reflect such interesting details, but they do show that the 1950 transfer from Hale to Gambill was valued at $20,000 and included substantially more property than was sold to Olerud.

Buddy Gambill, grandson of Vincent, does not recall family discussion of this particular transaction but does confirm that his grandfather was an aggressive gambler. "My granddaddy taught me how to play 'Pitch to the Line' and then liked to take money off me playing the game," remembers Gambill. "I also remember him playing a tough game of 'Go the Distance' [based on the city names on Coke bottles] at Crockers filling station." A high-stakes poker or dice game in the postwar years would not have been out of character for Vincent, according to his grandson.

Less is known of Hale, the alleged debtor, but land records show that in 1943 he owned almost sixty acres, including the store site. He transferred the store property in 1943 and got it back from a different owner in 1947. With five transfers in seven years, it could be that the store property was being tossed about as gambling collateral.

Indifferent to the property history, and with Mavis keeping the books, Olerud set about running the store and making friends. Two years later, the "tarpaper shack" disappeared, and Gil's Supermarket opened on the site. "A good size store in those days…and the first supermarket in Smyrna," recalls Ginny Williams, daughter of Gilbert and Mavis. Ginny, her sister Candy and their brother Gilbert were raised in the store "with a grocery cart for a play pen." When they were big enough to help in the store, they were

Gil's Supermarket built in 1955. *Photograph from the Olerud family collection.*

fitted with small aprons and put to work stocking, sacking and delivering. "We learned to size and repack the eggs, to slice slab bacon and to hack the chicken," explains Ginny.

"For Easter we colored chicks, and the ones that weren't sold we released in the trailer park," said Ginny. For Christmas, her father would dress as Santa and set up a chair in the store where the neighborhood children could present their lists. While Mavis handled the finances, Gilbert concentrated on marketing and promotions. Working with his close friend Mason Tucker at the *Rutherford Courier*, he developed annual event promotions such as a "Salute to Mothers" and the "Sam Davis Tribute." He knew how to compete with the big chains by promoting "loss leaders," and some Smyrna natives still remember buying five-pound bags of sugar for a nickel.

From the beginning, Olerud listened to his customers and worked to give them what they wanted. "For example, we stocked potato pancakes, special coffee brands and some of the first frozen pizzas, all in response to special requests from customers," says Ginny.

To increase beef sales, he launched the "Round-Up Days" promotion. All of the store personnel dressed in cowboy outfits, and a couple of quick-draw artists were hired to put on a show. Custom cutting of quality meats was a store specialty, and Ginny remembers that even regular commissary patrons on the air base would buy their meats at the supermarket. "Marvin Berry was one of the young butchers trained at the store," remembers Ginny. "One day, he cut off part of his thumb and we all had to look for it. We found it so we knew it wasn't part of anything we sold."

In 1960, a full-service garage and filling station was added to the family operations. In 1962 came the Skyway Drive-In, a hamburger and dairy dip operation featuring the "Big Ole." The Skyway Restaurant opened in 1964.

In 1970, the air base closed, and many worried about the future of Smyrna. Olerud's response was his plan to build the Gilsville Family Center, the first shopping center in North Rutherford. At the grand opening in 1973, he gave away a new car (the Vega, General Motors' answer to the fuel shortage). During this period when jobs were scarce, particularly for young people, Olerud kept as many as fifty on his payroll.

Gilbert Olerud died in 1980, but Gilsville continues as a family owned and managed business. All of the property is still owned by the children of Gilbert and Mavis, except for the street that now runs beside the original store and trailer park—Gils Street. Ginny manages the hardware store,

Candy runs the convenience mart and Gilbert does maintenance for all the properties.

"My father always said that he was building for his family and his community," says Ginny. Thirty years after his death, his legacy still provides for his family and serves his community.

PAINTER'S CAREER CAME TO A SHOCKING END IN RUTHERFORD

No one knew his name or recognized his face, but millions of travelers knew his work. He was a painter, perhaps an artist, and his contribution to the image and idiom of the American South was probably greater than that of any other American painter. His career, however, came to an abrupt end on July 11, 1968, in Rutherford County.

Clark Byers was hired in 1936 by Garnett Carter of Chattanooga to paint barn roofs without charge to the barn owner if the painting could include a message—"See Rock City!" Byers was sent out along federal highways around the South and Midwest to find high-visibility roofs and to convince barn owners to accept a free paint job with the advertising

A barn on the Manchester Pike, U.S. 41, in Rutherford County. *Artworrk by David Weigant.*

message. (A few Rock City trinkets and souvenir pictures were also part of the usual compensation.)

Carter had developed the concept of miniature golf, and during the 1920s, he accumulated a fortune franchising Tom Thumb Golf throughout the United States. While Carter was franchising tiny golf courses and developing a fashionable subdivision on Lookout Mountain near Chattanooga, his wife was landscaping and planting a huge rock garden around the rock promontory and cliffs on the east side of the mountain (near their own home). For her efforts, she was the first southerner to receive the Garden Clubs of America Medal of Distinction in 1933.

Carter sold the golf company in 1930 and turned his attention to his wife's garden. Trails were widened, suspension bridges added and statues of gnomes and storybook characters (which had originally been part of the Tom Thumb golf course décor) were added. The garden park was opened to the public under the Rock City name in 1933, at the depth of the Great Depression.

Despite intense commercial promotion efforts, the park languished as a local attraction for several years. Then Byers went to work. "I couldn't figure out how Carter could afford to pay me forty dollars a sign," said Byers in a 1990s interview with David Jenkins, author of *Rock City Barns* (Free Spirit Press, 1996). "But I went up to Rock City one day and the parking lot was full, and the signs had done it."

Being paid on a per-sign basis, Byers recognized the value of quick work. He hired a couple of assistants to blacken the roofs with his original blend of lamp black and linseed oil. On the following day, he would lay out the lettering and fill in the white while his assistants painted another barn. Working freehand with four-inch brushes, Byers was able to complete three to five signs a day when he was on the road. Not even Byers could say for certain how many barns were painted, but some sources have counted as many as nine hundred sites.

Falling off a barn was just part of the job. "When you start slipping, you start running and jumping over the wet paint to the lowest part of the roof—then you jump off," explained Byers. The worst part was spilling paint on the ground because you had to let it dry and then dig it up—"Kills the cattle, you know!"

By the 1960s, things were changing. The Interstate Highways had pulled most of the traffic away from the old routes where the barns were located, and the federal regulation of highway signs did not favor barn signs. As a result, Byers and his crews were painting more billboards. (Byers also is

Clark Byers, who braved charging bulls, slippery roofs and lightning bolts to paint "See Rock City" on barns across the South for three decades, died in 2004. *Photograph courtesy of the* Daily News Journal, *Murfreesboro.*

credited with the first use of the "See Rock City" birdhouse, which became the enduring symbol of the successful tourist attraction.)

On July 11, 1968, Byers was retouching the letters on a billboard seven miles south of Murfreesboro on the Manchester Pike (near the Buchanan/ Epps Mill Road intersection) when he made contact with the utility power line. "[The shock] set my hair on fire and burned a place on my back—it was a miracle it didn't kill me," said Byers in his 1990s interview. "I was in the hospital for a while and couldn't do anything for a year." That was his last work for Rock City.

Soon after the incident, Byers sued the Middle Tennessee Electric Membership Cooperative in federal court, alleging negligence. Jim Baker, retired CEO of the utility and a witness at trial, recalls that Byers had been using a roller brush on a long aluminum pole when he apparently contacted a distribution line carrying 7,200 volts. The jury found the utility guilty of ordinary negligence with respect to the maintenance and protection of its lines but denied Byers any recovery because of his own negligence in failing to exercise proper care for his own safety. (A finding that the injured party is guilty of "contributory negligence" prevents any recovery in Tennessee.)

On appeal, Byers attempted to get around the contributory negligence bar to recovery by arguing for a finding of "gross negligence" against the utility. The appellate court found no evidence that the utility had actual or constructive knowledge of a dangerous situation before the accident and denied the appeal.

Despite the shock and trial loss, Byers survived and prospered into his eighties. He developed Sequoyah Caverns, a tourist attraction in northeast Alabama, and ran a three-hundred-acre farm until his death in 2004.

Thanks to Dwight Stone and the Hoopers Institute for research assistance.

Rutherford Roots in Modern Romance Novel

"Scandalous" in their time, two women authors from Rutherford County—Mary Noailles Murfree and Bonnie Golightly—made unique contributions to the romance novel genre.

Murfree, great-granddaughter of Colonel Hardy Murfree, was born in Rutherford County in 1850, daughter of a prominent attorney. She was educated in finishing schools in Nashville and Philadelphia and spent her summers in Beersheba Springs, a resort community south of McMinnville, where her family owned a cabin.

During the 1870s, Murfree wrote and published a number of stories appearing in various national journals. Since it was at that time considered inappropriate for a lady, particularly a genteel lady from a "proper" family, to be engaged in journalism, Murfree wrote her first two articles—"Flirts and Their Ways" and "My Daughter's Admirers"—under the pseudonym "R. Emmet Cembry."

When the prestigious *Atlantic Monthly* published "The Dancin' Party at Harrison's Cove," a romance set in a summer resort modeled on Beersheba Springs, Murfree used another masculine pseudonym, "Charles Egbert Craddock." It was by this name that her writings became popular during the Victorian 1890s and the early twentieth century.

Before her death in 1922 in Murfreesboro, Murfree wrote over two dozen novels, including some historical fiction. Her favorite setting was a

The 1940 Come and Go Club members at the Tennessee College for Women pose with the car belonging to club president Betty Jackson. The local commuters are (left to right) Jackson, Wordna Bragg, Mary Lee Crouse, Ann Kirtley, Ellen Avery Carlton, Gladys Bugg, Sara Elizabeth Arnette, Margaret Groom and Martha Sims. Club vice-president Bonnie Golightly is not pictured. "Bonnie was frequently not where she was expected," remembers a classmate. *Photograph from the Tennessee College for Women Annual (1940).*

romanticized depiction of southern mountain life. Her novels have been consistently criticized, however, for her stereotyping of the mountaineer and for her highly romanticized descriptions of the landscape. In contrast, the writings of Bonnie Golightly rarely mention the landscape and make little use of historical details, but two of her books were made into movies, and her lawsuit against fellow novelist Truman Capote made national headlines.

Golightly graduated from Central High in Murfreesboro in 1937 and attended the Tennessee College for Women (TCW, 1937–40), where she was feature editor for the school newspaper, a member of the Craddock Club (theatre and drama) and vice-president of the Come and Go Club. Wordna Bragg Black, current president of the TCW alumnae association, explains that the Come and Go Club was for the local girls who daily commuted to the campus.

Bonnie was the daughter of Thomas J. Golightly, professor of education at the State Teachers College (now MTSU). During the mid-1930s, the Golightly front porch at 1212 East Main in Murfreesboro was a favorite gathering spot for teenagers. Among the porch crowd were C.B. Arnette and

The Golightly home with the popular front porch on East Main. *Photograph by Greg Tucker.*

Thomas B. Cannon, who remember Bonnie as the daughter of indulgent parents. "She was popular in part because she drove a blue Willys-Knight convertible coupe," remembers Arnette. "We gathered on her porch because we knew we were welcome there, and because there wasn't much else to do." Cannon remembers Golightly as "quiet…friendly with most of the boys, but not a heavy dater." Among her friends and contemporaries were Charlotte Ezell, Susan Lytle and Dorothy Jarrett. Black remembers that Golightly "pretty well did whatever she wanted." Her contemporaries had a few more parent-imposed restrictions.

During World War II, Golightly married a serviceman from "up north," and by 1950 she had moved to New York. Her first novel, a paperback published in 1957, was titled *The Wild One*. In classic pulp fiction style, the cover shows a barelegged blonde with a tease line: "Living it up was all fun and kicks—the hard part was living it down!" Three years and three novels later, Golightly collaborated with Paramount Pictures on *A Breath of Scandal* ("the glittering story of a fiery princess who scandalized an empire"). With a cover depicting another barelegged blonde, this time draped over an antique bed, this book was made into a movie directed by Carlo Ponti and starring Sophia Loren, Maurice Chevalier, John Gavin and Angela Lansbury.

Through a dozen or more novels, Golightly's heroines were all liberated, single women searching for adventure and romance. Compared to the graphic and explicit writings of today, Golightly's tales of intimacy are tame, but for her time she was clearly "on the edge," with titles like *Brat Girl*, *Wife Swappers* and *High Cost of Loving*. She knew success, however, for what appears to have been her last novel, *In Search of Gregory* ("a luxurious tapestry of deception and incest"), also made the screen in a Universal production starring Julie Christie.

Late in her career, Golightly collaborated on one nonfiction book (*The Problem-Solving Psychedelic*), which was in part a directory to popular drugs of the 1960s.

One unusual distinction—an AKC champion pedigree Australian shepherd was named Bonnie Golightly, and the name still appears on pedigree papers.

Some evidence of her lifestyle as a pulp fiction author is found in the lawsuit she filed in 1959 alleging that Capote invaded her privacy in his bestselling novel *Breakfast at Tiffany's* (also a very successful movie). She claimed to be the real-life original of Capote's heroine Holly Golightly ("a charming cornpone New York geisha"). The Capote character, she alleged, was based on details of her life gleaned from "mutual friends."

Described in media reports as a "twice-divorced blonde built along dinner-at-Schrafft's lines," Golightly never collected on her claims. However, in October 1998, her *New York Times* obituary described her as a "colorful New York writer thought to be the original of 'Breakfast at Tiffany's.'" She reportedly died after a prolonged stay in a New England sanitarium.

V

Traditions and Life

November Was Hog-Killing Time
in Rutherford County

On most Rutherford County farms a couple of generations ago, November was hog-killing time. Some folks just went by the calendar and used a specific date, like November 15, for the annual ritual. Others always made it part of their Thanksgiving week tradition. Some went by lunar phases: "You don't never want to kill on the new moon…you wouldn't get much lard and the meat would swell up. Kill on the full, or nearly full, moon."

Ralph Puckett remembers that his father, Gum Puckett, always killed on the full moon. "He said that there wouldn't be any red gravy if there wasn't a full moon," says Puckett. The practical approach was to kill after the first hard freeze when the weather turned cold to stay. Since most farms had no freezers, they had to rely on the winter weather to keep the meat from spoiling while it cured. (Many of us can remember when sixty-degree days were rare in November.)

"We did the work on a big, flat rock by the creek where there was a huge cedar tree," explains Puckett. "That spot was easy to clean up since the blood ran into the creek, and we hung the carcass from the cedar." Ninety-two-year-old Frances Brandon reminisces that when she was five, she was

Gum Puckett with wife, Mattie, and twins, Ralph and Ray. *Photograph from the Puckett family collection.*

told to stay on the porch during hog-killing so she wouldn't get blood on her bare feet and track it all over the house.

In early morning, the scalding water was readied, usually in a big, black iron pot set on stones over a wood fire. Puckett's job as a child was to keep the fire going. The hog was killed with a shot between the eyes.

140

(Some farmers kept a small .22 "hog pistol" primarily for this purpose. The low caliber at close range was a quick kill, affecting very little meat.) Immediately, the throat was cut: "Stick a flat blade in the goozle until the blood flows." (The jugular vein is severed on the left side of the throat about three inches back from the jawbone.) When the bleeding slowed, the hog was doused with scalding water to loosen the bristles. While the men started another hog, the women and "young 'uns" would scrape with a dull knife, repeatedly scalding as needed, until all the hair was off the hide.

Ray Tenpenny recalls that his family used a fifty-five-gallon drum and dipped the carcass. If the water was too hot or the carcass was

A "hog pistol" (Remington vest-pocket .22) used by four generations of a local farm family for slaughtering hogs. *Photograph courtesy of the* Daily News Journal, *Murfreesboro.*

immersed for too long, the hair would "set" and have to be tediously plucked. Another method was to wrap the carcass in burlap and pour scalding water over the cloth. "Then you could rub the bristles off with the burlap," explains Tenpenny.

The carcass was then hung with a stick and pole between the hind legs and the head removed. After the remaining blood drained from the carcass, a long cut was made down the middle of the underside "from crotch to chin," the large intestine was cut free and tied shut and the entrails were dropped out into a large pail. The liver, lungs, heart, kidneys, stomach and small intestines—and even the head, feet and blood—were often saved for food or other uses. "We fed it all back to the hogs," says Puckett. "They'll eat anything." A sausage pot would be readied for lean trimmings and a lard pot for the skin and fat trimmings.

"I REMEMBER THE hog killing at Uncle Billie's on the Bradyville Pike. Several families would bring their hogs to his place and all helped each other. What a nice thing to do," writes Sam Woods. "I think helping each other is a thing almost gone."

Leaf lard (fat from the abdominal cavity) was removed and put in the lard pot while the carcass was still hanging. When the inside of the carcass was completely clean and a long cut had been made down the back to the bone, the carcass was taken down and cut up. Using an axe, the ribs were cut off both sides of the backbone. The tenderloin was removed and usually cooked fresh within the next few days. Shoulders, hams and side meat were trimmed out for curing (four to six weeks in salt, depending on the weather). The trimmings were put in the sausage or lard pots. Ribs were trimmed and chopped into two- to three-inch sections for canning, as was the backbone.

With a little spring water added "to get it started," the lard pot was boiled for several hours until the clear, liquid lard separated from the skin and fat fiber. According to Frank Grimes's recollection, it was ready "when the cracklins start to rattlin'!" The pot contents were then poured into cloth and pressed with homemade "lard squeezers" to wring out the clear liquid lard, which hardened as it cooled. What was left was "cracklins," which were used in bread making, turkey stuffing and other country dishes.

Sausage making was a creative activity, and every family had its own traditions and recipes. Hand-cranking the sausage grinder, however, wasn't easy. "To keep me going," says Tenpenny, "Momma would start cooking some of the fresh sausage while I was grinding. That smell, and the promise of hot biscuits and sausage, was enough to keep me working."

POPULAR CHRISTMAS CAROL ORIGINATED IN LOCAL MILK BARN

Oh, beautiful Star of Bethlehem, shining afar thru shadows dim.

A tenant dairy farmer in the Plainview community, Robert Fisher Boyce, walked across the road to the milk barn in 1938, sat down on a milk stool and drafted the lyrics for a new hymn, which he titled "Beautiful Star of Bethlehem." Describing his experience as a work of "divine inspiration,"

Boyce later explained that the "beautiful star" described in his song was the person and spirit of Jesus.

After a week of revising and refining the lyrics, Boyce worked with his pianist daughter, Nannie Lou Boyce (Taylor), to put the lyrics to music. For the next two years, however, the song was heard only in the Boyce family and in the neighborhood churches where Boyce sang or led congregational singing. Members of the Mount Carmel Baptist Church on Manchester Pike, where Boyce was a deacon, remember that Boyce and his wife would sing the song together and that she would cry every time she sang her husband's song.

Although unsuccessful in his initial efforts to get his hymn published, Boyce was not a music novice. Twenty-five years earlier, at about the time of his marriage to Cora Carlton, Boyce wrote a hymn entitled "Safe in His Love," which was published by the Showalter firm, the nation's leading publisher of religious music in the early twentieth century. Also, since his youth, Boyce had performed with gospel quartets in churches and at revivals around Rutherford and surrounding counties. For many years, he led the annual all-day singing program at the Old Leb Methodist Church near Midland.

In 1940, Boyce attended the Vaughan Normal School of Music in Lawrenceburg, Tennessee. The James D. Vaughan Music Company was at that time the world's largest publisher of "shape note" songbooks. Shape notes (literally musical notation using seven different shapes for the scale tones) were first developed in the late eighteenth century for use in teaching singing to frontier church choirs and congregations. But by the early twentieth century, shape note singing had evolved into a gospel style that was hugely popular in the rural churches of the American South, although it had largely disappeared elsewhere. (Though shape note singing may not be as common today as it was prior to the 1950s, there are still many churches in the rural South, particularly Primitive Baptist and Churches of Christ, that regularly use shape note songbooks.)

Recognizing the growing popularity of shape note singing in the southern states, James D. Vaughan established his firm in centrally located Lawrenceburg and promoted his songbooks by sending salesmen quartets to churches to entertain and sell books. By the 1920s, Vaughan also owned the Lawrenceburg newspaper, a radio station and a local bank and was the town mayor. Alger Pace, a baritone in the Vaughan Radio Quartet, was hired to edit the songbooks and head the music school (yet another means to promote shape note singing and sell songbooks).

While a student at the Vaughan school, Boyce showed his composition to Pace, and a partnership emerged. Within a few months, "Beautiful Star of Bethlehem" was included in the Vaughan songbook. The copyright owner,

142 Beautiful Star Of Bethlehem

Copyright, 1940, Pace and Boyce, owners.

Adger M. Pace. Theme by R. F. B.   R. Fisher Boyce. Har. by A. M. P.

1. Oh, beau-ti-ful Star of Beth-le-hem, shin-ing a - far thru shad-ows dim,
2. Oh, beau-ti-ful Star, the hope of light, guid-ing the pil-grim thru the night,
3. Oh, beau-ti-ful Star, the hope of rest, for the re-deemed, the good and blest,

Giv-ing a light for those who long have gone, have gone; And guid-ing the wise men
O - ver the moun-tain till the break of dawn, the dawn; And in - to the light of
Yon-der in glo - ry when the crown is won, is won; For Je - sus is now that

D. S. - Oh, give us thy light to

on their way un - to the place where Je - sus lay,
per-fect day it will give out a love-ly ray, Beau-ti-ful Star of Beth - le -
Star di - vine, brighter and brighter He will shine.

light the way in - to the land of per-fect day,

FINE CHORUS

hem shine on.   Oh, beau-ti - ful Star   of
    shine on.   Beau-ti - ful, beau-ti - ful Star,

D. S.

Beth - le-hem,   Shine up-on us un-til the glo - ry dawn;
   Star of Beth-le-hem,   glo-ry dawn;

however, was not the Vaughan Company. As noted on the songbook page, the copyright was held by "Pace and Boyce, owners." The songbook credited Boyce for the "theme" and Pace for the harmony. What role Pace played in shaping the published version of the song is unclear, but some contemporary sources credit him with the musical composition. (Pace's online biography also credits him with a dozen other hymns.)

After completing the Vaughan school, Boyce traveled the region teaching "singing schools" and selling songbooks for the Vaughan Company. In 1954, Boyce gave up milking and opened a grocery store at 914 West Main in the Westvue community of Murfreesboro. Soon thereafter, Boyce began selling a sheet music version of the song for "50c EACH." The credit line on the sheet said "By Pace and Boyce," and the song was reprinted exactly as it appeared in the Vaughan songbook. The sales address on the sheet music was the Boyce grocery store in Murfreesboro.

It appears that Boyce retained the sheet music rights but gave songbook and performance rights to Pace as an agent for the Vaughan Company. Shortly before his death, Boyce apparently transferred his copyright ownership to the songbook publisher. The current copyright was assigned to the James D. Vaughan Company in 1967. The Vaughan catalogue of songs and copyrights is today owned by Spirit Sound Music Group, based in Cleveland, Tennessee.

For several decades, the song remained a favorite hymn in many southern churches but had little exposure to a wider audience. Over time, it came to be used as a Christmas hymn, although this was not the author's intent. Sometime after Boyce's death in 1968, the song was "discovered" by popular music fans and performers. Professional recordings and performances began with the John Daniel Quartet at the Grand Ole Opry and now include recordings by Emmylou Harris, Ricky Scaggs, Bill Gaither, Ben Speer and the Judds. In the last decade, "Beautiful Star of Bethlehem" has become a standard in gospel Christmas albums by several publishers, including Daywind Records (2001), Melody Trio (2004) and Mount Harmony Records (2006).

A memorable performance, enjoyed by daughter Nannie Lou just before her death, was a White House performance by Naomi and Wynona Judd as part of a Bob Hope Christmas special in 1993. Shortly afterward, Naomi wrote to the family describing "Beautiful Star of Bethlehem" as "not only our favorite all time carol, but a reminder of the most magical time in our lives [when she and her two daughters had each other and little else]. Music helps us keep memories alive."

"WHITTLE CLUB" PERMITTED ONLY
SHAVINGS AND TALK

If you are a serious practitioner, you know that the blade must be honed to the correct angle, the cedar stick has to be properly cured, the grip has to be right for delicate control and you have to be able to concentrate on the task while listening and talking about unrelated affairs of men and state. Such is whittling.

Michael Horine is a master woodcarver who lives and works at the southeast corner of Highland and Lytle in Murfreesboro. As seen in the yard, his work products are useful and/or artistic. He obviously carves with some purpose or objective in mind. For the dedicated whittler, however, there is rarely any intention regarding a useful or artistic end product. The only intent is in the activity itself—reducing the stick to long, slender shavings with no preconceived use or purpose.

Carving is a solitary occupation. Whittling, however, is best practiced as a social or group avocation—or so it was some sixty years ago, when the Murfreesboro whittlers' club included some of the area's more prominent professionals and businessmen. They convened during the lunch hour to discuss the issues of the day, to reminisce about what had come before and to taunt and tease one another in a good-natured exercise of friendship—and also to whittle.

"It was against the rules to make anything other than shavings," recalls eighty-nine-year-old J.T. Burnett, the sole surviving member of the 1940s "Whittle Club." Burnett was one of the youngest club members. "I was there through the courtesy of Claude Harris, my dentist and business partner," explains Burnett. "I was new to the area after the war, but they all accepted me into the group because I was the son-in-law of Charlie Bailey, owner of the popular Ideal Barbershop behind the bank on Maple Street."

Lunch for several of the whittlers was usually taken at Bessie Shipp's Wagonwheel Café in the Mason Court Building at the corner of East Main and Spring Streets, across from city hall and "just down from the chamber of commerce." Elsewhere in the building were several medical, insurance, real estate and law offices. City Attorney Alfred B. Huddleston and his partner, Clarence Cummings, brother of a governor and a successful trial lawyer, were on the second floor.

One Main Street door opened into a hallway through the building. Past the stairway and through an inner door was the clubroom. Nothing fancy—a bare light bulb on a ceiling drop cord, coat hooks, exposed pipes, electric meters and switch boxes. In the corner to the right was a restroom, and a back door opened to a parking lot and shaded backyard near the Jordan Apartments.

Following the midday meal, the whittlers would congregate in this hallway, seated on various straight-backed chairs. The chief adjudicator of this informal club was W.T. "Will" Henderson, an osteopath with his office in the Mason Court Building. He was a serious whittler who set the standards—sharpening the knives for those who needed help and furnishing the cedar sticks. (Henderson was also a flower breeder who raised prize gladioluses.)

Henderson's technique, copied by the more skilled in the group, dropped no shavings as each sliver was left hanging at the end of the stick. Nevertheless, a broom stood prominently in the corner ready for the inevitable end-of-the-hour sweep out. "I wasn't much of a whittler," admits Burnett, "and I never could get the fuzzy stick thing. I often did the sweeping." Burnett also frequently enjoyed the talk and camaraderie without a pocketknife.

Dr. Harris shared a medical/dental office with Henderson and was often responsible for a good-natured laugh at the expense of a fellow whittler. Two other dentists were Ben Patton and T. Warren Garrett. Patton was rumored to have invested in the restaurant business out of state but would speak little of it. Lawyer Wiley Holloway, one of the younger whittlers, was for a time the local district attorney and a serious golfer. Paul R. Lynn, an optometrist, was a two-fisted whittler who let the shavings fall.

James Moore King and Robert Alvis Huddleston were among the opinion leaders in the group. King was a real estate dealer and investor with offices in the Mason Court Building. Huddleston, a political ally and close friend of Congressman Albert Gore, commanded the local company of the home guard during World War II and ran an insurance business from offices in the same building. King was the respected elder in the group, just ahead of Henderson.

Two of the youngest members of the group were Walter Early and Burnett. The latter, with financing from Harris, was in the tombstone business, selling and engraving. He was usually distinctively dressed in a one-piece work suit but always over a dress shirt and tie. Early, whose whittling followed the style of Dr. Lynn, was a dental apprentice with Dr. Harris in 1948 but soon moved to Florida.

The yard behind the building had two large shade trees. "If the weather was good, we would each pick up a cane-bottom chair and head out the

Members of the "Whittle Club" in 1948 were (left to right) Walter Early, Dr. T.W. Garrett, J. Moore King, Dr. W.T. Henderson, R.A. Huddleston, Dr. C.C. Harris, Dr. Paul Lynn, Wiley Holloway, Dr. Ben Patton and J.T. Burnett. *Photograph from the collection of Robert Huddleston Jr.*

back door," recalls Burnett. "The activity always ended abruptly when they blew the one o'clock whistle at the Carnation plant, and we all went back to work."

A 1948 photograph of the group shows the styles of the day—only the two youngest are without hats. Senior members of the group are in three-piece suits with watch chains across their vests. (And we thought only men in overalls spent their time whittling!)

Thanks to Bobby Huddleston and Bubba Woodfin for research assistance.

CAMPING ON STONES RIVER WAS A 1920S FAMILY VACATION

Everyone around here was healthy, prosperous, friendly and having a good time in 1924, according to the perceptions of an eight-year-old vacationing with family and friends in Rutherford County. The annual family vacation was an extended campout on the bank of the Stones River on the Edmondson farm. The perceptions were those of retired educator and area native Frances Brandon.

The Edmondson farm on the west bank of the river at the mouth of Stewarts Creek had been in the Edmondson family for several generations. By 1916, the original lands had been divided between Robert Edmondson, H.R. Edmondson and the widow of T.P. Edmondson. (Most of the farm is now beneath the waters of Percy Priest Lake, but portions are still accessible east of Jones Mill Road in LaVergne.) The campsite was close to the widow's home, which was just west of the creek mouth. The campout began with the Fourth of July and continued into August, with family and friends coming and going. Stays ranged from days to several weeks.

For Brandon and her four-year-old sister, the fun began with loading the car. The old Dodge had no trunk, so the backseat was piled high with clothes, bedding, food, cooking utensils, fishing gear, lanterns, hunting equipment, cots and every manner of camping essentials. On top were tied the tents and tarps, crib, cane fishing poles, washtub and anything else that would not fit inside. The two sisters squeezed in amongst the items on the backseat while their father drove and their mother rode up front holding the baby.

The route was through Smyrna and then due north along Stewart Creek. The last part of the drive was across fields and gullies to a level area in a river bend where the water ran from shallow on the camping side to quite deep in the middle and along the opposite bluff. Near the campsite, a cold spring emerged from a small cave (big enough to play in).

During the camping season, the field to the back of the campsite could have anywhere from three to a dozen vehicles. "Mostly Fords, except for our old Dodge," remembers Brandon. Family names among the campers included Moss, Ellis, Ransom, Sweeney, McLaughlin, Grimes, Williams, Earls, Shelton, Bugg and Coombs. "We were all related or close friends. There were lots of children."

Family housing was in large canvas or cloth tents, some home stitched, with tie lines and stakes. Tent poles and stakes were found or cut in the surrounding woods. Grass floors soon were worn to earth, and lighting was kerosene lamps hung from the ridge pole. Some of the short-stay campers slept in bedrolls on the ground, but most families had canvas cots stretched on wood frames. Brandon and her sister shared one cot, arranged with heads at opposite ends, but that alignment never lasted through the night.

This and next two pages: Camping on the Stones River in the 1920s. *All photographs from the Shelton family collection.*

Although sleeping was by family (except for sleepover kids), the feeding was done banquet-style. "The men set up a long table that was actually planks on stumps or hand-tied sawhorses. Probably could set two dozen or more on whatever you had to sit on," explains Brandon. Many brought chairs and stools; others made them from whatever was available. Cooking was done on an old, abandoned wood stove that someone had hauled in and set on rocks and on an open fire ring that was kept hot for baking and boiling water.

Foods included ham, fish and small game (rabbit and squirrel), fresh garden fruits and vegetables, chicken and eggs, some wild plants, a few store

treats and a daily bread bake. The farm families usually sent one of the men home every other day or so to tend to the livestock and such, and this worked well for resupply, since he would return with fresh garden vegetables (squash, cucumber, okra, tomatoes, corn and beans) and with fruits (plums, apples, peaches and pears). "Several families brought chickens in crates for fresh eggs, and I doubt that any of the hens ever went back home," recalls Brandon.

The children and women picked dewberries. (The dewberry is a trailing variety of blackberry that once flourished in parts of the county. The ground-hugging runners could grow out ten or twelve feet making for easy picking without the briars.) "Mama would fill a pastry shell with fresh dewberries; sprinkle sugar, salt and flour over the berries, dot with butter, and bake in a covered pan in hot coals," remembers Brandon. "There was never enough."

A pond back on the farm was choked with cattails, and Ms. Edmondson encouraged the campers to dig out the edible roots. Cleaned and ground into a mushy gruel, the root was sun-dried, mixed with egg, milk, butter or margarine and a little salt and cooked as a pancake in a well-greased cast-iron skillet. "This was a treat served with berries or fried apples for breakfast." There was always skillet cornbread, and every afternoon someone would bake sugar cookies.

Several families would bring and share home-cured ham, and one grocer friend always brought a quantity of link sausage, bologna and other specialty meats. "Along with the fish we caught, and some occasional game meat or fowl, we had lots of variety," says Brandon. "Seems like there was always a ham slow-cooking in a lard stand." Brandon observes that "if there wasn't cooking, there was washing—pots, pans, utensils, clothes, dressed fish, babies—something was always getting washed."

Fishing was both an individual and an organized activity. Two flat-bottomed rowboats were rented from local farmers, and every evening several trotlines were put across the river. The campers took turns running the lines in the morning and bringing in the catch. Later in the morning, the children would help with seining for bait, and before nightfall the lines were re-baited. "We caught a lot of catfish, carp and a few suckers. Sometimes there would be a turtle on one of the lines."

Everyone fished—some for food, others for fun and some as serious sport.

My father was serious about his fishing. I remember his cane poles. They were Tennessee white cane that he found and cut personally. The big end would be close to an inch thick with a taper to about three-sixteenths of an inch at the tip. He hand-fitted each pole with glass-lined metal eyes and crank reel brackets taped in place. The tape and cane were heavily varnished for durability and waterproofing. With live or cut bait, a cork bobber, hook and shot weight, I caught at least one pan-sized bluegill every day. Hellgrammites were my father's favorite bait, but they pinched me. [Hellgrammites are the aquatic larvae of the dobsonfly.]

Swimming and playing around the water were favorite activities for both children and adults. "We also made a game of gathering firewood by building forts and cabins of the dry logs and sticks." Mussel gathering was another activity for both children and adults. The children collected and played with the colorful shells. Some of the men opened hundreds of fresh mussels looking for freshwater pearls. "They would always find a few. I remember one fellow showing off a tie pin set with a pink mussel pearl."

The nearby cave spring provided fresh water but also served for refrigeration. "Two or three times a week, someone would drive into Smyrna for supplies, including a big block of ice." Wrapped in burlap and stored in the spring cave, the ice would last for several days helping to cool the milk, butter and other perishables. It also was chipped for icing drinks. "Depending on who went to town, the Smyrna trips could also mean candy in small paper bags for the children."

The evenings, after supper and cleanup, were always special. A group of black musicians from the neighborhood would often come into camp and play for tips. Brandon remembers the banjo, harmonica, other string instruments and a homemade drum that was played with open palms. Familiar hymns usually prompted good harmonies from among the campers. "They would always play 'Home on the Range' for the children."

Some of the young folk enjoyed square dancing, and a large tarp was stretched tight and staked down over hard ground to make a dance floor.

> *One of my uncles was a great jig dancer. Someone would always ask him to dance, and he loved to show off. I always giggled because he would make funny faces at us while he danced. No matter how fast or slow the music, he always stayed on beat. Some of the children would try to imitate his steps, and sometimes he would grab me or my sister to dance with him.*

The children were always sent to bed at a reasonable hour. When all the young ones were down for the night, the adults would put all of the lanterns on or above the big table and break out the playing cards. Some played Rook. "I liked the cards because of the blackbirds." Others played Pitch, and sometimes the children would hear one of them say loudly, "High, low, jic-jac and game!"

"I loved the night sounds—the whippoorwills, bullfrogs, crickets, peepers and tree toads, and the sound of the running river," remembers Brandon. "I also loved the low murmur of the adult conversations, and the occasional bursts of laughter. For a child, this was heaven."

Every evening, as the card games began, Ms. Edmondson would walk down to the river camp, leaning on her cane, expecting a glass or two of "iced tea." After consuming her "tea" and exchanging talk with some of the campers, she would walk back to her house, usually with assistance from one of the other ladies. "Many years later I learned that the tea was a rather strong mix of tea or juice and locally distilled whiskey," reveals Brandon, "but I do not remember anyone ever appearing to be drunk or tipsy, except maybe Ms. Edmondson."

Saturday night was when the ice cream was churned. The men took turns on the hand crank. "My favorite flavors were peach and strawberry, flavored with fresh fruit from local farms. Peppermint made with crushed candy was also popular."

On Sunday, the campers went to church—morning and evening. "My family headed up the road to the nearest Baptist church," confirms Brandon. "Most of us were Baptist, but several went to some of the other churches. It was expected that we would all observe the Sabbath, and we always carefully packed and protected our Sunday garments."

DEAD CAR, SMALL CROWD HIGHLIGHTED
MacARTHUR VISIT

Fired as the supreme military commander in the Far East by an unpopular president, General Douglas MacArthur returned to the United States in April 1951 as a war hero with realistic presidential ambitions—until he came to Rutherford County, Tennessee.

His Rutherford connection was Mrs. MacArthur, the former Jean Marie Faircloth. Daughter of a wealthy and socially prominent Rutherford family, granddaughter of a Confederate army captain and graduate of Soule College in Murfreesboro, for thirty-four years she was attended by a bevy of servants as she shuttled between the family mansion at the corner of Lytle and Highland Streets and the family resort in Estill Springs.

As a young woman, Jean Marie was the traveling companion of her divorced banker father as he traversed the globe in pursuit of business and personal interests. Travel became her passion and principal activity, as her father and a growing circle of international friends hosted and accompanied the attractive and intelligent Jean Marie on cruises and across continents.

On a cruise to China in 1937, the single, thirty-five-year-old Jean Marie met the divorced, fifty-seven-year-old MacArthur and his elderly, but still domineering, mother ("Pinkie"). He was on his way to Manila to assume his first Far East assignment. Romance blossomed quickly, and Jean Marie shortened her stay in China to accept an invitation to visit MacArthur in Manila. Returning to Tennessee, Jean Marie began immediate and secret plans to marry and relocate to the Philippines. On the pretense of visiting relatives in Louisville, Jean Marie met and married MacArthur (who was briefly in the United States for his mother's burial) and returned to the Far East.

Fourteen years and two wars later, with world attention focused on her husband's conflict with President Harry S Truman, Jean Marie returned to the United States and announced that one of her first stops would be a visit to her hometown with the general and their fourteen-year-old son. On April 23, local leaders learned that the visit would be on the couple's wedding anniversary—April 30.

Thrilled by the prospect of being the focus of world attention, and shocked by the short notice, the political, civic, business and social forces of the county quickly mobilized. The news media predicted that 75,000 to 100,000 people would swarm through the county to see the popular and controversial military hero and presidential aspirant.

Concerned that traffic jams in this rural area would impede the delivery of pictures and news copy to wire services, media representatives arranged for an airlift from the college airport to Nashville. College flight instructor Bobby Huddleston was hired to fly news material over the traffic to Nashville. Local committees were quickly formed for every purpose. Murfreesboro mayor Jennings Jones even appointed a committee to oversee the committees. The undertakers organized to provide a squad of ambulances to handle casualties trampled by the expected mob. John "Bubba" Woodfin recalls spending the day of the visit as one of the designated ambulance drivers.

Entrepreneurs saw opportunity in the need for food and refreshment for the anticipated throngs. Jake Warden took several days off from work to make sandwiches. Like many others, he staked out a spot on the parade route for his stand (he had a prime corner in front of Central High on East Main Street). The plan was for a motorcade to travel from Sewart Air Force Base to ceremonial locations in Smyrna and Murfreesboro and then to lunch at the Stones River Country Club. Roy Byrn, local car dealer, was the MacArthurs' driver in a 1934 Rolls Royce borrowed from a Columbia owner.

Veterans and civic groups took the lead in planning events. The United Daughters of the Confederacy (UDC) decorated the Civil War monument on the square in honor of Jean Marie's mother, a former UDC president. The statue and much of East Main were decked out in Confederate flags. An umbrella magnolia was removed from the courthouse lawn to provide a clear view of the monument.

On Sunday before the visit, the *Daily News Journal* published an eight-page "souvenir edition" detailing the lives of Jean Marie and the general. The virtues of Rutherford County were also identified through ads and stories. The lead story told of Jean Marie's rearing and the important role of "Mammy" ("a real *Gone with the Wind* type of mammy" who was a "second mother" to Jean Marie). The story featured pictures of the Lytle Street mansion and "Mammy's Cabin" behind the house. (All were later demolished for hospital parking.)

The day started well. A small crowd of state and Nashville dignitaries greeted the MacArthurs at Sewart, where Mrs. Ben Hall McFarlin presented flowers on behalf of the local women's organizations. The motorcade stopped first at the War Memorial in Smyrna for a wreath laying ceremony and then proceeded to the Haynes Hotel (later demolished) in Murfreesboro, where the general was made a lifetime member of the local Veterans of Foreign Wars (VFW).

Rear seat: General MacArthur, his son and Jean Faircloth MacArthur. *Front seat*: Murfreesboro mayor Jennings Jones and car dealer Roy Byrn. *Photograph from the Rutherford County Archives.*

As the motorcade circled the square, the Rolls Royce died and the UDC monument was ignored. Several volunteers pushed the car to Jones Field on the MTSC (now MTSU) campus. (A picture of the presidential hopeful being pushed along in a dead auto might have been prophetic, but only one vague reference to an "uncooperative" vehicle and no pictures appeared in the media.)

At the James K. Polk Hotel, Mrs. Ed L. Jordan presented flowers on behalf of the local Daughters of the American Revolution. Hotel owner John Harton announced that a plaque would be permanently placed on the building to memorialize the historic occasion. (The hotel was subsequently demolished. SunTrust Bank is now on the property.)

As the motorcade pushed its way out East Main, it was apparent that thousands had not come to cheer for MacArthur and his family. A later account noted that only "hundreds lined the parade route." The disappointed food vendors gave most of their sandwiches and treats to friends and charities. The news media airlift never got off the ground. Not a single ambulance pickup occurred. Although in brief remarks the general promised, "I shall return" for another visit, he was never seen again in Rutherford County.

Historical note: In 1952, MacArthur's rival, Dwight D. Eisenhower, was elected president, and today historians rank MacArthur's nemesis, Harry S Truman, as one of our five "greatest" presidents. The general's place in history remains controversial at best.

STORIES TOLD BY FENCES: FEUDS, PSYCH CARE AND PERSONALITIES

Even the fences tell tales in Rutherford County, Tennessee.

Devil's Fence

Virgil Pitts and Ellis Peyton, neighbors on Trimble Road in the eastern portion of Rutherford County in the 1940s, raised sheep.

Their respective sheep pastures shared a common fence, and for years they fumed and fussed at each other about maintenance of the fence and

Steve Blankenship stands against the original pasture fence. One court-ordered fence is seen in the foreground. Twelve feet back (marked by ribbon in the center of picture) is the parallel fence ordered by the court. *Photograph by Greg Tucker.*

whose animals were running in which pasture. They could distinguish the animals since one farmer removed the tails and the other didn't.

Eventually, three ewes with tails were found on the wrong side of the rather porous fence, and their tails were cut. Before long, the neighbor recognized his missing livestock despite the missing tails. As would be expected, sharp words and not so idle threats were exchanged, and the matter wound up in general sessions court.

Clearly, the court was more concerned about the long-running "fence feud" than the status of three sheep. The judge apparently wanted to emphasize that folks would be a lot better off if they would get along and work together. He ordered each of the parties to build a new fence the length of their common property line and paralleling the existing fence at a distance of six feet. A sheriff's deputy was detailed to confirm compliance with the order. This new fencing created a twelve-foot "dead zone" straddling the length of the original fence.

Steve Blankenship, raised on a neighboring farm, remembers hearing that each of the mandated fences extended for about one mile and "cost more than the value of either herd." Neighbors took to calling it a "devil's fence." A section of the triple fence can still be seen on the east side of West Trimble Road about fifty feet south of the 4978 mailbox.

Window Bars

In 1976, C.B. Arnette purchased from a scrap metal/junk dealer in Beech Grove a quantity of iron window barriers recently removed from the patient buildings at the Veterans Administration (VA) psychiatric hospital north of Murfreesboro.

The iron sections, approximately two by four feet of ornamental iron, were used to protect the hospital windows and to prevent entry or exit when the windows were open. Specifically, they were to prevent patients from falling or climbing out the windows. Apparently, with the advent of

This iron fence on the Lebanon Highway is made of the window barriers removed from the Veterans Administration psychiatric facility in the 1970s. *Photograph by Greg Tucker.*

"chemical restraints" (drugs), it was decided that the window barriers were no longer required. Gail Norton, who worked for many years as a VA nurse, remembers that removal of the iron barriers was a "policy decision" relating to public perception of the facility and its programs.

Joe Dill welded the sections into four-foot squares, which were joined to make a decorative iron fence across the two-hundred-foot front of Arnette's fifteen-acre residence on Lebanon Pike. The fence still stands at the corner of U.S. Highway 231 North and Cherry Lane.

Great Wall of Rutherford

Beulah Hughes was said to be the only Republican in Rutherford County in the middle years of the twentieth century. She was a Tennessee delegate to several Republican National Conventions in the days of Dwight Eisenhower and Richard Nixon.

Her home was just east of the geographic center of Tennessee on what is now the Old Lascassas Pike. The farmhouse sat between the road and the old rock quarry. The place was sold to John T. Cunningham, a prosperous local optometrist, in the 1970s. The eye doctor's politics were not noted,

This decorative wall on Old Lascassas Pike was built for the eye doctor who liked rocks and heavy equipment. The pattern of the surface rock indicates a concrete block infrastructure. *Photograph by Greg Tucker.*

but neighbor Robert Stroop recalls that Dr. Cunningham was fascinated by heavy equipment. "We were doing some building and excavation shortly after he moved into the neighborhood, and on some days he would stand at the fence and watch the heavy equipment work for an hour or more."

Eventually, Cunningham bought himself a backhoe, and for his birthday his wife gave him a Caterpillar DH dozer. He had no training or experience on the equipment but enjoyed pushing and scraping dirt and rock around the old quarry. "One day we noticed that he had scraped and leveled a strip along the pike and down each side of his new house," remembers Stroop.

Cunningham hired some of the Baxter clan. (Five or six generations of the Baxters have been master stonemasons, including Ray Baxter, who taught his sons the trade after being blinded and losing one hand in a dynamite accident—but that's another story.) Using stone gathered from all over the county, they built for the doctor the most imposing yard enclosure in the county. "I guess he also liked rocks," muses his neighbor.

You can still see the wall just past the geographic center monument on Old Lascassas Pike.

Teenagers, Bah!

The first Central High School building in Murfreesboro was opened in 1919 next door to the Maple Street home of James A. Moore, a wealthy

This brick wall behind the 1935 Central High football team was built in the 1920s to isolate the Maple Street residential property from the new high school. The wealthy homeowner did not want the students on his property. *Photograph from the Tucker family collection.*

builder reputed at the time to be "the only infidel in Rutherford County." He didn't like teenagers, particularly the ones who walked across his property. He bought the lot between Maple and Walnut Streets and demolished the former home of John C. Spence, founder of the original cedar bucket factory in Murfreesboro, in order to build his own "modern" residence. Soon after classes began at the new high school site (now the Murfreesboro Housing Authority), Moore built a high, rough stone and brick wall that served as a visual screen, as well as a barrier to foot traffic.

The Walnut Street portion of the wall remains behind the former Discovery House (now a law firm office).

Romantic Rutherford Runaways Remembered

You elegant fowl! How charmingly sweet you sing!
O let us be married! How long we have tarried.
—"The Owl and the Pussycat," 1871

Getting married, always a memorable experience, can take a lot of forms, ranging from a formal church wedding with the air of a high social function and hundreds of guests to a simple pronouncement by a local judge. But according to *The Modern Fable* (1901), "If it were not for the Presents, an Elopement would be Preferable." Webster's defines "elopement" as "running away secretly, especially in order to get married." A couple of Rutherford County examples are illustrative.

Rural Route Romance

The August 4, 1908 entry in the diary of Readyville rural mail carrier J.V. Cates says simply, "The fatal day," notes Steve Cates, grandson of the mail carrier. Bessie May Carnahan lived with her parents and siblings on what is now called "the old McGill place" near where the Cripple Creek Loop road now intersects the new Bragg Highway. J.V. Cates delivered the Carnahan mail, and romance blossomed. But Bessie was only twenty, sixteen years junior to her sweetheart. Moreover, her family was Church of Christ; his was Baptist. Anticipating family objections, they exchanged notes in the mailbox.

Joseph (Jody) and Bessie Cates. *Photograph from the collection of Lee Saupe.*

The elopement plan was set. On the night before the "fatal day," Bessie hurried her younger siblings through the evening chores and off to bed so she could prepare for the morning events.

Early the next morning, Bessie slipped out of the house while her family slept. She met her fiancé at the mailbox. They went by buggy to the home of Squire L.B. Bowling at the corner of Ringwald Road and the Woodbury Pike. A squire (a corruption of the more formal "esquire") in those days was an elected member of the county court, the legislative and governing body for the county (predecessor of the county commission). Under state law, the squires (also called justices) had not only legislative duties but also certain judicial and executive powers, including the authority to conduct misdemeanor trials, arraignments and marriages.

After a quick marriage, Bessie and her new husband drove the wagon to the Murfreesboro depot and boarded the morning train heading to Louisville, Kentucky. Meanwhile, Bessie's brother Burton came to the home breakfast table in tears announcing, "Bessie's gone!" Realizing what had happened, Bessie's father, A.L. Carnahan, walked down the drive and tearfully called to the neighbors that "Bessie's gone and married old Jodie Cates!"

The newlyweds honeymooned in the home of Jodie's brother, Aubrey Cates, a prosperous Louisville lawyer. The Cates home had gaslights. When Jodie put out the light on the first honeymoon night, he blew out the flame as he would on the oil lamp back home. Smelling gas, brother Aubrey hurriedly interrupted the newlyweds to turn off the gas and explain the hazard.

Not until four years later, after the birth of the second grandchild, did Papa Carnahan finally visit in the home of Bessie and Jodie.

Flight to Ringgold

Recently returned to Rutherford County from World War II service in the South Pacific, Ed Lowe was courting Kathleen Todd in 1946 when he was offered a job with the Civil Aeronautics Administration (predecessor of the Federal Aviation Administration). The job was based in Atlanta, and he had to be on the job by the following Monday. Not wanting to leave without Kathleen, and knowing Kathleen would go only as his wife, Lowe proposed a brief stop in Ringgold, Georgia, on the way to Atlanta. By the 1940s, most states had imposed licensing requirements and a waiting period for marriage (blood tests were also standard). The State of Georgia, however, did not adopt a waiting period or residency requirement and set the age of consent at fourteen.

As a result, the town of Ringgold, the aptly named first stop in Georgia on the Dixie Highway, became known for "fifteen-minute marriages, no waiting." Numerous "wedding chapels" lined the highway through Ringgold and prominently advertised a romantic and memorable "quickie marriage," complete with license, blood test and a keepsake photo.

Ed and Kathleen were confident that both families would favor their marriage, but they also expected that the Todds, prominent and substantial landowners known throughout Rutherford, would insist on planning and conducting an elaborate garden wedding with friends and extended family gathered for the special occasion.

Kathleen enlisted her youngest sister, Marie, as an accomplice and maid of honor. "We gave her a round-trip bus ticket for Ringgold." On Saturday morning, July 7, Kathleen hired a taxi driven by a former boyfriend, Bill Petty. "I snuck out with a small suitcase, dropped Marie at the bus station and met Ed at the college [now MTSU] airport," recounts Kathleen. "I didn't run away. I flew away, and I was scared to death having never before been off the ground!" The plane was a two-seater Vultee BT-13

Ed and Kathleen Lowe. *Photograph from the collection of Ed and Kathleen Lowe.*

Valiant that Ed bought from war surplus. "I thought he was rich—he had an airplane!"

"We flew to Chattanooga, hired a cab, picked up Marie at the bus station and headed over the state line to Ringgold." According to the bride's recollection, the whole process—license, fee and vows—took about fifteen minutes. "The cab waited. After the wedding, we took Marie back to the bus station and checked into the Read House in Chattanooga for our honeymoon. On Sunday we flew on to Atlanta."

Four moves and twenty-four years later, the Lowes moved back to Rutherford County. "My twin sister, Christine, was still mad at me for not including her in my wedding."

Gum's Catalogue House Still Standing on Rutherford Farm

John A. Gum bought a fine and fancy new house in 1913. It was delivered to his Rutherford County farm in pieces—some assembly required. He lived in it for the rest of his life, except for several years in prison.

The Gum house was one of the early ready-to-assemble homes sold through mail order by Sears, Roebuck & Company. During the years from 1908 to 1940, it is estimated that between 75,000 and 100,000 Sears catalogue homes were sold in North America.

In 1906, Sears managers were looking for a way to boost sluggish sales in the catalogue company's building materials department. Frank Kushel from the porcelain china department suggested to Richard Sears that the company assemble kits and sell entire houses through mail order.

By this time, the Sears catalogue was a standard in millions of American homes, and folks had become accustomed to ordering products sight unseen from the thick volumes. The company had established a reputation for quality products and customer satisfaction. Also, because of its owned production facilities, low store overhead and large volume, Sears was usually able to underprice local retailers.

In 1908, Sears bought a lumber mill, began assembling home building kits and issued its first specialty catalog featuring twenty-two house styles priced from $650 to $2,500. Each home kit included plans, specifications and all

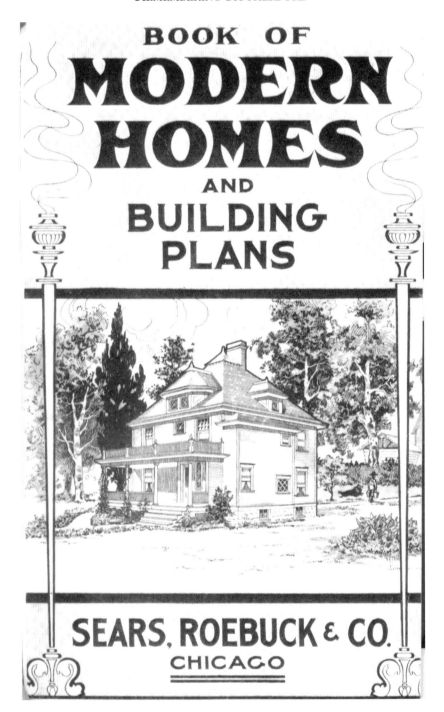

This 1908 mail-order catalogue offered ready-to-assemble homes from Sears, Roebuck & Company.

The catalogue home bought and assembled by Frank Gum on his Manus Road farm in 1913. On the porch are Sallie Jernigan Gum (seated at left, wife of Frank Gum), her son Dewey Gum (seated at right) and granddaughter Dorothy Jean Gum. Circa 1940. *Photograph from the collection of Michael Stanley.*

materials. Also offered was financing, assembly skills, sequencing instruction and guarantees. The first home was delivered in 1909.

By 1912, Sears owned three lumber mills and a millwork plant devoted to producing mail-order homes. Ordered by mail and shipped by rail, the material shipments were sequenced and timed to meet a six-month building schedule "from the ground up." Sales increased steadily and "boomed" in the 1920s (a fourth lumber mill was opened in 1925). After the 1929 market crash and through the Depression, however, catalogue home sales sputtered. The catalogue offering of homes ended in 1940.

Although Sears offered popular and established styles and materials with little innovation, the catalogue homes were among the first to feature standardized and precut framing, drywall as an alternative to lathe and plaster and asphalt shingles. Most of the catalogue homes are still standing, and the Rutherford County home at 8006 Manus Road clearly evidences the material and design quality that was promised and delivered almost one hundred years ago.

The 144-acre Manus Road farm had been in the Gum family for several generations when John A. Gum decided to dismantle the 106-year-old, two-story log house and replace it with a new Sears catalogue home. The first materials were delivered in July, and the construction was completed in December 1913. Most of the work was done by Gum, his family and a few hired hands. According to family records, the catalogue price was "about $600."

The house is Folk Victorian style with four gables, two long porches, a patterned metal roof and swan neck adornments on each roof peak. The original colors were off-white with green trim and a gray roof. The framing and wood trim are yellow poplar. Original amenities included fireplaces and outdoor plumbing.

Gum (a cousin of Frank Gum, father of movie star Judy Garland) was known to be a skilled builder. Joe D. Allen remembers when his landlord hired Gum in the 1940s to do stone masonry work. "Mr. Gum could build most anything," remembers Allen. "I was just a child and knew nothing of Mr. Gum other than the work he was doing, but the hard look in his eye was scary. Whenever he came to the house, I would hide." But Allen also remembers a rare kindness. "He hand-carved a beautiful rolling pin and gave it to my mother."

Gum and his family—his wife (the former Sallie Jernigan), their four children and his mother (Martha James Benson Gum)—settled into their comfortable new home in the winter of 1914. Although Gum had purchased the property interests of his siblings after his father's death, his mother had retained a "life estate" in the property. As a result, under the law Gum had only a "remainder interest" in the property.

The family's "quiet enjoyment" of the property ended in November 1925, when Gum's nephew-in-law, Grady Jernigan, killed neighbor James E. Merritt and Merritt's oldest son. Gum was convicted as an "accessory before the fact" and given a life sentence. Grady was convicted as the hit man and also given a life sentence.

Faced with a $3,000 bill for legal services from E.C. Holloway and Wilkes Coffey, Gum signed two-year promissory notes using his interest in the farm and house as collateral. In 1927, the notes were in default, and Holloway & Coffey took possession of the collateral (Gum's remainder interest). But because of Martha Gum's life estate, the use and actual possession of the property did not change.

By the time Gum was released in the late 1930s, having served the minimum time for a life sentence, his wife and children had paid off the

The catalogue home today, looking much as it did in 1914, is now the home of Michael and Alecia Stanley.

lawyers. (Mrs. Gum also gave her nephew a home on the family farm after his release.) Gum resumed his farming and construction work and lived in his unique house until he was committed to institutional care in 1951.

After her husband's death, Sallie Gum sold the farm and house in 1952. Four owners later, the original catalogue house still stands, looking very much as it did when it was first occupied in 1914.

Unique Buick Brought Auto History to Discovery Center

On Wednesday, August 13, 2008, the Discovery Center opened the "Wheels" phase of its new Transportation Gallery. Featured in the midst of the "hands-on" displays for the children is a gleaming, Brass-era beauty—a 1910 Buick Model F Tourer. A gift from the collection of Ed Delbridge, this automotive treasure is a most appropriate representative of the early history of the American automotive industry.

A 1910 Buick Model F Tourer. *Artwork by David Weigant.*

The first automobiles appeared in the 1890s, and during the early decades of the twentieth century there were many entrepreneurs trying to capture this emerging market. In Tennessee, they made Marathons in Nashville. In Detroit, Michigan, a plumber named David Buick decided to apply some of his fortune and inventive genius to this fledgling industry. Buick had earlier developed the process for annealing porcelain to iron and amassed a fortune selling bathtubs and sinks. His inventive genius in part involved hiring talent who knew more than he did about automobiles. Among his engineers and craftsmen were Charles Nash, Walter Chrysler, William Durant and Louis Chevrolet.

Buick introduced the Model F in 1907, and for the next four years Buick was the market leader. With a two-cylinder gasoline engine mounted under the front seat, a rear-wheel chain drive and a two-speed transmission, the Model F was the style and technology leader of the period. (If you are wondering, the fuel tank and radiator are under the front hood.)

Buick sold his interest in the company, leaving only his name, before the Model F production run ended. His exit from the industry may have been prompted, in part, by the "cheap" car that fellow Detroiter Henry Ford began producing in 1908. In any event, Nash, Chrysler and Chevrolet soon became competitors. Durant stayed with the Buick company and eventually built it into General Motors. It's no wonder that "Detroit" came to be synonymous with the American automotive industry.

Back in Rutherford County, the Byrn-Reagor Motor Company had the Buick franchise, but by 1920 it had added the Chevrolet line in an effort to meet the Ford competition. Earthman-Wilson-Elkin Motor Company, a Murfreesboro tractor and farm implement dealer, had expanded into automobiles with a Ford franchise a few years earlier.

But the Discovery Center Buick did not come to Murfreesboro through the Byrn-Reagor dealership. The ownership history of this particular vehicle began in upstate New York.

The first owner got the Buick for fifty cents—the cost of the winning raffle ticket at the 1910 county fair in Syracuse, New York. The elderly winner drove his new car a bit to show it off and then put it on blocks in a shed for the winter. (At that time, a car was not useful transportation during a Syracuse winter.)

Before spring, the owner died of influenza. He was survived by two sons, who feuded over ownership of the Buick while the car remained on blocks. Several decades later, one son died, and the survivor decided that the car had caused too much dissension and grief to be kept in the family. He remembered that Sam Manton, as a child in the neighborhood, had frequently played in the car, so he called Manton in Florida and said, "If you will come and get it, you can have it!" Manton immediately flew to Syracuse and claimed the car. Back in Florida, Manton cleaned off decades of neglect, did minor maintenance and was soon showing off his "like new" 1910 Buick.

In the early 1960s, Delbridge, a prosperous Murfreesboro photographer and apartment developer, and his wife, Clara, were touring Florida in a Chevrolet convertible, towing a trailer with the idea of adding to their already impressive antique car collection. Delbridge met Manton, a fellow Antique Automobile Club of America (AACA) member, who at the time was looking for a "good home" for his vintage Buick. Impressed by the car's original condition and incredibly low mileage (less than one thousand miles), Delbridge paid the asking price and brought the car home to Murfreesboro.

"Mechanically the car is all original—even the upholstery and spare tire are factory original," says Delbridge. "When I decided to put the car in national competition, I had it professionally repainted." In its national debut, the car fell just short of perfection because one judge found a

DESCENDANTS OF GUM Puckett remember him telling that the first automobile seen regularly on Bradyville Pike was a T-model Ford driven by Hendrick Woods, the local veterinarian in the years before and after World War I. Puckett claimed that every horse along the pike was spooked by the passing car, or maybe they ran because they knew it was a vet.

small crack in the radiator. When next entered—with the radiator repaired—the Buick was the 1986 AACA National Award winner. In 1992, it won the AACA Grand National Award.

The care and maintenance of the rare Buick is now under the supervision of Ralph Puckett, chairman of the Discovery Center's automobile advisory panel. "Anybody involved with antique cars knows Ralph," says Delbridge, "and nobody knows more about old cars than Ralph Puckett."

CENTURY-LONG EFFORT REQUIRED FOR FULL VOTING RIGHTS

The right of citizens of the United States to vote shall not be denied or abridged…on account of race, color or previous condition of servitude.
—Fifteenth Amendment, U.S. Constitution

The Thirteenth Amendment to the United States Constitution, the Emancipation Proclamation, dramatically changed the social and economic fabric of the Old South in 1865, and the Fifteenth Amendment significantly recast the political terrain.

As local political autonomy was restored following the Reconstruction era, elected officials in Rutherford County, and throughout the southern states, recognized that the new black vote was potentially a significant factor in local elections, but early efforts to attract this new bloc of votes were awkward and usually unsuccessful.

In 1929, local historian and publisher C.C. Henderson recounted the story of one such effort by Murfreesboro mayoral candidate Ervin Burton in 1882. Burton identified Hardin Ridley as an opinion leader in the local black community of that time.

In an effort to advance his candidacy, Burton approached Ridley with a request for assistance in lining up support among the black voters. Assuming that Ridley would expect to be rewarded for his efforts, Burton offered "a jug of the best whiskey to be had for his services." Ridley agreed and asked for specific instructions. Burton explained that Ridley should assemble the prospective voters and then "call the meeting to order and remain in the chair until it was adjourned."

After all had been assembled, "Burton took the promised whiskey to the rear of the hall" and notified Ridley of the location before departing, leaving matters to his newly recruited political operative. What happened thereafter is recounted by Henderson:

> *Hardin Ridley took the chair and promptly called the meeting to order. As soon as order was obtained, Hardin then as promptly announced that the caucus stood adjourned...* [and] *retired by way of the rear door taking the jug of whiskey with him. He contended afterward that he had complied with his part of the agreement in both letter and spirit.*

By the beginning of the twentieth century, a generation after Burton's ill-considered effort, black voters across the South were subjected to intimidation, fraudulent promises, payoffs and official obstacles to exercise their vote. According to *The International Encyclopedia of Elections* (1999), the poll tax (a tax to be paid as a precondition to voting) was one of the most effective obstacles.

A one-dollar poll tax was implemented in Tennessee in 1889, consistent with the 1870 Tennessee Constitution:

> *All male citizens of this State, over the age of 21 years...shall be liable to a poll tax of not less than fifty cents or more than one dollar per annum. Nor shall any county or corporation levy a poll tax exceeding the amount levied by the State.*

Rutherford County took advantage of the "local option" and added one dollar to the state levy. The financial burden of the tax was significantly enhanced because it was cumulative. (If a voter missed voting for five years, his tax obligation for the next election would be six dollars.) Also, there was the inconvenience of paying the tax at a specified location, often months before the election, and then preserving the documentation for presentation at the polls.

In the 1930s, the Tennessee Democratic Party advocated for repeal of the poll tax, and Prentice Cooper campaigned against the poll tax in 1936.

No. 1408 **POLL TAX RECEIPT.**
RUTHERFORD COUNTY, TENN.

Murfreesboro, Tenn. ... 191

Received of ... *the sum of*

... DOLLARS,
100

in full for POLL TAX for the year 1915, in District No.

Trustee.

$ ...

By ... *D. T.*

McQUIDDY PRINTING CO., NASHVILLE

POLL TAX RECEIPT
No. ... RUTHERFORD COUNTY, TENN.

Murfreesboro, Tenn. MAR 1 - 1919 191

Received of ...

the sum of ... DOLLARS,
100

in full for Poll Tax for the year 1918, in District No. ...

Trustee.

$ ... *By* ... *D. T.*

MARSHALL & BRUCE CO., NASHVILLE

After his election, however, Cooper failed to press for repeal. During this period, Rutherford County repealed its local portion of the tax. Perhaps the "last straw" was in the postwar 1940s, when the Crump political machine in Memphis started buying large blocks of poll receipts and distributing them to lower-income supporters. In 1953, the Tennessee Constitution was amended to end the state poll tax.

In 1964, the Twenty-fourth Amendment to the U.S. Constitution banned poll taxes for federal elections, and in 1966 the U.S. Supreme Court used the Equal Protection Clause to ban any tax as a prerequisite to voting in state and local elections. With voting rights guaranteed, and with court-mandated reapportionment leveling the rural/urban playing field in state and local politics in the late 1960s, the ranks of the elected began to reflect a true voter profile.

On July 8, 1968, the Rutherford County magistrates' roll call included Isabell Killgo and Johnie Murray representing the newly defined Thirteenth District (Murfreesboro). Four years later, experienced educator Ola Hutchings was the first black member of the Rutherford County School Board. At her first meeting on September 7, 1972, Hutchings successfully advocated a plan for providing special education services. She died during her first term on the board and was eulogized by board chairman Roy Waldron for her "many years of service as a teacher...for her leadership...for her advocacy for her people...for her integrity, sense of justice, and fairness...not only a credit to her race but more importantly to this community."

Dora Rucker, a fourteen-year veteran of the Rutherford County Election Commission, remembers the county's first two black magistrates (now called commissioners). "Mrs. Killgo was an attractive and successful businesswoman, very active in her church and community." She ran the Killgo Funeral Home at 301 South Academy and operated a second business making drapes and upholstery. Murray was a popular barber with a shop on State Street and a reputation for "helping his neighbors." The community remembers and appreciates the role and commitment of these "early pioneers."

VI

Crime, Scams and Fights

Ghouls Once Profiteered in Rutherford County

It was nearly midnight when the Sweeney brothers finished stringing trotlines across the creek mouth one summer evening in the waning days of the nineteenth century. They were walking back across the Bryant place in the bright moonlight when they heard a wagon coming down the gravel road (now the Couchville Pike) at a fast pace.

Out of both caution and curiosity, the boys waited beside the road for the wagon to pass. As it flew by, they saw three men crowded together on the bench seat. One of the men, wearing rough work clothes with a hat low over his eyes, held the reins and urged the horse on when he saw the boys. The man in the middle sat up straight, staring ahead and wearing what looked like a white shirt, a coat and a tie with no hat. The third man was dressed like the first, with a hat nearly hiding his face. He had one arm around the shoulders of the middle passenger.

"Did you see the fellow in the middle?" Mort asked his younger brother after the wagon passed.

"Yeah, he was kind of dressed up," responded Howell.

"He was dead!" exclaimed the elder.

Artwork by Minh-Triet Tucker.

What the brothers had witnessed was criminal activity that reached its peak in the 1890s—grave robbing and trafficking in corpses.

Following the Civil War, the practice and teaching of medicine changed rapidly with the expanding knowledge of the anatomy and physiology of the human body. Anatomy instruction required corpses or cadavers for dissection and study, and the occasional availability of an unclaimed criminal or pauper's body failed to meet the needs of American medical schools. Besides, the medical schools preferred relatively fresh cadavers, as opposed to those that had been stored long enough to be deemed "unclaimed." On the supply side, most families of that era believed that only "proper burial" was acceptable, unless the deceased happened to be a criminal or pauper.

The medical school trade was not the only incentive, however. Ransom, sideshow display and jewelry theft also motivated some of the desecrators. Notable attempts to steal famous bodies for ransom include those on the remains of poet Ralph Waldo Emerson (1889), New York financier John Jacob Astor (1890), showman P.T. Barnum (1891) and perhaps the most brazen scheme—President Lincoln (circa 1870). The body of Lunalo (the "barefoot king of Hawaii") was successfully stolen in 1899. His venerated remains were sold piecemeal to islanders as good luck charms.

Bodies of dwarves and those with birth anomalies were popular in the sideshow circuit. They were usually shipped out of country to avoid recognition and seizure. Theft of valuables from ancient graves had gone on for centuries but took on a different character when grave robbers (often called "ghouls" in contemporary media reports) targeted fresh graves. These ghouls encountered some unique risks. A Peruvian smallpox victim was buried in 1891 with her wedding rings. Within hours, the body was exhumed and left exposed with rings removed. Local authorities hurriedly reburied the remains on the following day, but within the next few days, the body was twice again exposed by ill-informed robbers. This criminal activity was given credit for a village-wide outbreak of the disease. On the more positive side, grave robbers in Minneapolis in 1895 were credited with unintentionally rescuing a man buried alive.

Most of the grave robbers were independent entrepreneurs, but not all. Five students and two faculty members from the Kansas City Medical College were convicted of robbing graves in 1895 to supply the school's anatomy lab. Locally, there was Eagleville physician C.B. Hiemark, whose motive was simply money.

Hiemark came to Eagleville in the mid-1890s, allegedly from Vanderbilt Medical School, and built a good practice, despite what some of his neighbors described as "peculiar behavior." He was said to be of "Norwegian extraction," medium height, with "a walk like a coon's." He boarded in the McGowan home but also rented a small shed just outside town that he kept locked.

Hiemark paid Young Jody McGowan and a "Negro boy" for some odd purpose not initially suspected. It involved periodic trips to Nashville "in a wagon hauling mysterious bundles." Hiemark would get a change of horses in Nashville and return to Eagleville by morning, ready to practice medicine.

Hiemark's medical practice continued for three or four years, and only with hindsight did Eagleville residents realize that a suspiciously high number of his patients who were not critically ill died soon after receiving treatment.

GRAVE ROBBERS ARRESTED, BODIES RECOVERED

C.B. Hiemark, MD, had an active practice in Eagleville in the 1890s, but it was not until the discovery of two open graves that the community began to understand just what activity the doctor was pursuing.

One day in 1897, Henry A. Gee, gravedigger and cemetery caretaker, noticed a swatch of gray hair on a barbed-wire fence near the Russell Cemetery (near the North Main and Oak Streets intersection). This prompted the discovery of two open graves. The missing remains were those of Eva Jane Ornean Corbitt, the recently deceased wife of Richard Corbitt, a farmer on Shoemaker Road, and a Mrs. Pruitt (various reports provide no other identifying information).

Eagleville-area grocer Charles P. Gillespie heard from local hack driver Bill Elmore that someone had "dug up" the bodies of two women recently buried at the Russell Cemetery. This information reminded Gillespie that some of the local children had recently reported that the Bennett Cemetery grave of his late father-in-law (Steve Bennett) had a "sinkhole" in it.

When Gillespie checked the Bennett grave, he found the coffin box sticking out of the ground. "The coffin was in it, but they had taken the body, stripped it and left the clothes," recounted Gillespie. (The Bennett Cemetery is near the intersection of Highway 99 and Mount Vernon Road.)

Steve Bennett Jr. personally contacted Governor Bob Taylor and requested help while relating the gory details of this outrageous crime. The governor ordered an immediate state investigation. State troopers began by searching the medical school in Nashville without result. Meanwhile, the body of Mrs. Pruitt was found abandoned in the woods near Eagleville. It appeared that the robbers, fearing exposure, had dumped the body.

Dr. Hiemark quickly became the target of suspicion as his neighbors and the state investigators focused on his "peculiar" night trips to Nashville. Pat Hanafin, a detective working with the state troopers, traced the Corbitt and Bennett bodies to an address in Burlington, Vermont. They had been shipped there from Nashville in a box marked "Books."

The investigation by Hanafin and Rutherford County sheriff J.J. Lee revealed that an "eastern concern" had contracted to pay Hiemark forty-five dollars for each body delivered to it. The "eastern concern" was apparently serving as a broker, selling bodies to eastern medical schools for dissection in anatomy studies.

Although the Bennett, Corbitt and Pruitt bodies were the only ones proven to have been desecrated by the doctor and his two hirelings (Young Jody McGowan and an unidentified "Negro boy"), it was acknowledged that the doctor had been practicing and acting "peculiar" for a number of years. (A number of other Eagleville-area graves of that period may contain no remains.) In hindsight, some of his Eagleville neighbors also speculated that the doctor's patients who did not appear to be critically ill, but who had died soon after receiving treatment, might have actually been poisoned in furtherance of the doctor's side business.

Hiemark was arrested and arraigned before Squire R.S. Brown and indicted by the local grand jury in February 1898. Convicted of the misdemeanor of "disinterring a body for an unlawful purpose," he was given six months in jail and fined $150. Lacking the forensic tools of today, there was no evidence to support the suspicions of homicide, and only the misdemeanor charge was adjudicated. Young McGowan, an accessory to the crime, apparently cooperated with the authorities and, consistent with public opinion, was not charged. The Negro boy fled and was never captured or charged.

Photograph by Greg Tucker.

The Hiemark case attracted statewide attention and prompted the legislature, in 1899, to make grave robbing

a felony punishable by imprisonment in the penitentiary for a period of not less than two or more than five years for any person who removes any dead body or disinters any dead body from its place of interment for the purpose of selling or otherwise disposing of same to any person, company or corporation for the purpose of dissection or otherwise mutilating said body without first having obtained the consent of the family or relatives of the deceased.

The Bennett and Corbitt bodies were returned to Rutherford County by train, and according to the *Nashville Banner*, "There hasn't been such a country gathering since the day the bodies arrived in Murfreesboro." They were met by two horse-drawn hearses, and a huge crowd followed

In the August 2009 issue of the Rutherford County Historical Society newsletter, editor Susan Daniel tracked C.B. Hiemark, MD, through census and medical society records as follows:

1903: Fergus Falls, Minnesota, private practice
1904: Wendell, Minnesota, board of health chairman
1907: Elbow Lake, Minnesota, coroner
1910: Akeley Township, Minnesota, general practice

He does not appear anywhere in the United States in the 1920 census.

the hearses back to the respective cemeteries, where they were reburied in unmarked graves. (The Pruitt body had already been reburied at the Russell Cemetery in an unmarked grave.)

For a long time after the Hiemark experience, folks around Eagleville kept close watch over their recently interred dead. It was a common sight to see lanterns hanging around fresh graves.

So what became of Hiemark? He paid his fine, served his time and, in 1906, was again practicing medicine, according to the *American Medical Association Directory* (vol. 1, 1906), in Battlelake, Minnesota.

"BLACK GOLD" HOAX SETS UP FARM SWAP

We all know about "salting" food for preservation or consumption—particularly pork shoulders and hams. But "salting" has another meaning, according to Webster's dictionary: "To give a false appearance of value by fraudulent means."

Now, most local folks around here have never had the inclination or the opportunity to "salt" mines or properties to flimflam a neighbor—except for Henry Clark.

In the 1870s, Clark owned a farm in the hills southwest of Eagleville near the origin of Spring Creek, although the spring itself was on the neighboring farm owned by the Johnson family. The two farms had been partitioned fifty years earlier from the fifteen-hundred-acre plantation of William Logan, son-in-law of James Henderson, one of the original settlers in this region.

The partitioning for distribution to the Logan heirs was carefully achieved to give nearly equal value to the respective heirs. Accordingly, although the spring was on the Johnson property, the boundary between the two tracts was set so that the stream from the spring ran across a corner of the Clark farm, thus ensuring a good supply of water for each tract. Clark, however, coveted the few acres of rich bottomland around his neighbor's spring.

After the death of Josiah Johnson, the Johnson family patriarch, Clark began plotting to get the rich bottomland from the surviving widow and children. His clever plan would cost him just a few dollars.

To appreciate the cleverness of Clark's scheme, one has to understand that rural property values in the 1870s were based almost exclusively on agricultural productivity. The only other occasionally significant factor was mining potential, and Tennessee was then one of the largest producers of "black gold" (bituminous coal).

Coal was essential to virtually every major industry of the post–Civil War industrial era—manufacturing, transportation and urban heating. Although the known Tennessee coal fields in the 1870s were several hundred miles to the east, some local folks still believed that coal beds might exist in some of the more remote sections of Rutherford County.

One of those "remote sections" was in the northeast corner of Clark's farm. The terrain there was so steep that you had to hang onto the trees to get across it. The soil was thin and rocky, and the rocks were full of what looked like seashells.

On the sly, Clark went to town and bought a small wagonload of lump coal, which he then scattered over about ten acres of the steep hillside. When the "salting" was complete, and figuring that a discovery by someone other than himself would be more credible, Clark sent some of his farm hands into the remote area for hunting or timber cutting.

Soon, rumors began to circulate about what might be in the ground on that particular slope.

Photograph by Greg Tucker.

185

Courthouse records do not show who made the first offer to buy or sell, but on July 9, 1877, two deeds were filed in Rutherford County. The deeds show that the Johnson family traded thirteen and a quarter acres of bottomland to Henry Clark in exchange for ten and three-quarter acres of hillside property on the northeast corner of Clark's farm.

Surely the deception was eventually recognized, for no coal was ever mined on the property, but the swap transaction was never undone. Today, the Clark farm is still intact and is owned by the Dyer family. The current eastern farm boundary is still consistent with the Logan partition, except for about ten acres of steep hillside off the northeast corner and the addition of about thirteen acres of pretty bottomland at the southeast corner.

Did Henry Clark live "happily ever after" with his new bottomlands? Not quite. It seems that Clark ran up about $3,600 in debts secured by personal notes. The notes were eventually acquired by Young Redmond, an aggressive "notes trader" based in Franklin.

In 1883, Redmond got judgment on the notes and sought a forced sale of the Clark farm to cover the debt. Clark quickly "sold" the farm to his sons and argued that the farm was not reachable to satisfy his personal debts. The Chancery Court in Franklin ruled, however, that Clark's sale was a sham and ordered that the farm be sold to pay off the notes. Clark appealed to the Tennessee Supreme Court. Before the appeal was decided, Clark died sitting in his rocker on the front porch of his farmhouse and was buried on the property.

The Tennessee Supreme Court finally ruled against the Clark heirs in 1891, but the ghost of Henry Clark is probably still enjoying those thirteen acres of pretty bottomland.

County Clerk Prosecuted Schoolhouse Brawlers

J.P. "Jim" Leathers served as Rutherford County Court clerk for thirty-three years (1919–52). He was a proud man who expected an appropriate measure of deference and respect. He also considered himself a skilled auctioneer and handy with the ladies.

Leathers "campaigned" year-round by volunteering his services as an auctioneer for charity bazaars, fundraising events for various women's clubs,

The Burks Hollow School held classes from 1847 to 1946. The old school building was replaced in 1920 with the current structure, which now houses the Hattie's Chapel Baptist Church. The church was named in honor of Hattie Youree McNabb, who taught in Burks Hollow in the early twentieth century. *Photograph courtesy of the* Daily New Journal, *Murfreesboro.*

school picnics and church homecomings. A favorite format was the box supper auction, where the ladies—particularly the young and single ones—would prepare a picnic dinner for two and seal it up in a decorated box to be sold at auction. The winning bidder not only got the box and contents, but he also got the privilege of sitting with the preparer for the picnic dinner.

"Mr. Jim" never declined an invitation to preside at a box supper auction. If a particular box looked promising, and the lady looked nice, he might even put in his own bid. One warm, summer evening in about 1935, such an event took place at the Burks Hollow Schoolhouse.

Burks Hollow is about as far as you can go and still be in Rutherford County; it's a remote southeast corner near where Cannon, Coffee and Rutherford Counties meet. To get into the hollow, folks used to drive their teams and Model Ts up the creek bed. Later, someone built a road up and over the steep hill at the west end of the hollow. It's one of those hills where the young farm boys learned the hard way that a mule team and most tractors can pull up the hill more than they can hold back going down.

At the east end of the hollow is a cave that provided pure and sweet drinking water for many of the hollow residents. Someone ran a pipe way

Mack Jernigan (Andrew Matthew Jernigan) was my paternal grandfather who died about the time I was born. I had always been aware of his bootlegging business, but it wasn't something my dad really discussed with me. I had played in the old barn on the "hill farm" many times as a youngster but was never aware of the secret. My dad and uncle Jim built the barn per my grandfather's plan when they were only thirteen and sixteen years old. It was destroyed in a freak tornado some years ago, but I did a watercolor painting of it as a Christmas gift for my dad back in the 1970s, and following his death in 1994 my mother gave it back to me. It was an unusual-looking barn with what Dad always described as a cantilevered roof. Mack was said to have a natural gift for architectural design and reportedly designed a number of structures, particularly barns, for other residents of the area.

The original part of the hill farm was a Revolutionary War land grant to the Jernigan family. My dad, local golf pro Woody Jernigan, and uncle Jim owned the farm jointly until the late 1970s, when Dad sold his half to Uncle Jim. It was inherited by my first cousin, James W. Jernigan Jr., when Uncle Jim died several years ago. Family lore has included stories about the "hainty holler" on the farm where the Ku Klux Klan hanged a white man for abandoning his large family and whose ghost is said to haunt the place. I stumbled on this part of the farm many years ago on one of my many camping trips there, and I must admit that it is quite spooky.

The "Old Man" Luke Jernigan mentioned in your piece had a son, Burt, and a daughter, Laurel, who married my dad's sister, Mary

back into the cave and brought the water flow out to a concrete trough at the edge of the road. During the Depression, the bottomland along the creek grew a few crops, and goats pastured on the steep hillsides. If you had a good no. 6 Hillside "Sy-Q," you might even get a decent hillside corn crop.

The most profitable endeavor in the hollow, according to the late William Roy Arnold, was the Jernigan still. Mack Jernigan kept such an inventory that he built a big barn with a hidden storage room behind a false wall. From either side it looked like a divider wall, but it was actually two solid walls with about twelve feet between.

If you climbed the steep road at the east end of the hollow, you'd eventually come to the road that ran from Bradyville to Gossburg. There were lots of good, honest, hardworking folks, a few rough ones and a number of pretty girls in and around the hollow.

The schoolhouse picnic was a major social event, and the hollow folk were all there. Quite a few came from over the hills as well, including some of those "rough" Bradyville boys. (The gossip was that one or all of the three Jernigan girls were the attraction.) All were in high spirits as Leathers readied for the auction. The boxes were put on display, and the women gathered nearby. The crowd and the warm weather prompted many to stay in the yard. The school windows were wide open so all could see and hear the proceedings. Several of the younger boys were designated to deliver the boxes and collect money from the winning bidders. "I was collecting dimes," remembers Frank Grimes.

As the evening progressed, Leathers was in top form, and the school fund was prospering. He even got some of the older fellows to bid up their own bid. No one was surprised that a number of husbands bid generously for the box prepared by their respective spouses.

Attention was, of course, focused on the competition for

Lou, and his brother, Jim. Uncle Burt passed away last month after turning one hundred in May. My cousin James and his wife took the article you wrote to Community Care of Rutherford County, where he was a resident, and read it to him. He was very alert for his advanced age, and they said he thoroughly enjoyed this article. He told them that the big brawl at the schoolhouse actually started over the box supper of my aunt Elizabeth. Dad's three younger sisters—Elizabeth, Vera and Catherine—were real lookers. I mean movie star beautiful. Elizabeth and Vera are still living in Michigan, although both have Alzheimer's disease.

Again, I thoroughly enjoyed your column, and so did my siblings and cousin James. I always enjoy your historical glimpses of life in the county in years gone by, but this one in particular struck a cord since we know so little about our dad's family of origin. If you have any other stories about them, we'd so love to hear them. Thanks again.
—*Nettie J. Monday, Lascassas, Tennessee*

the boxes from the young, single ladies—Ruth Reed, Elizabeth McCrary, Frances and Willie Beth Herrod, Louise Arnold, Ruby Bowman, Evelyn Ford and others. Roy Arnold bought the box fixed by Ophie Reed. The Jernigan boxes brought in a shower of dimes.

When all of the boxes were bid out, folks settled down to the eating and socializing. In the back of the schoolhouse, unsuccessful bidders, most of the Bradyville boys and several others gathered and began passing around a bottle or two. The trouble began when Jess Stillman (from up on "the ridge") stepped on the outstretched foot of "Old Man" Luke Jernigan—but it might have been Jernigan who did the stepping. Anyway, one complained and the other said: "Put your d--- foot in your pocket!" Fists started flying, and Luke hit the floor. Jess later recounted that Luke "just lay there like a stiff hoss."

This exchange was the trigger, and suddenly the back of the school exploded, with furniture, fists, bodies and bottles flying everywhere. James Bethel, the schoolmaster, rushed to break it up and went down on the first punch. Leathers backed up to the front wall and started "taking names." Most of the noncombatants went out the windows.

John O'Neal got up on a table and was "pecking others on the head" with his folded pocketknife "like a rooster pecking corn," recalled Arnold. Uncle Hardy Brewer grabbed Frank Lowe and shouted, "Frank, the old man's got you!" The younger Lowe swung around, grabbed Uncle Hardy's coattail and slung his elder into a corner.

As the fight progressed, parents rushed to get the younger children out of harm's way. Heard above the ruckus was the cry through a window: "Where's little Twiller, where's poor little Twiller!" (The mother of Aquilla Bowman, later a county squire and school board member, spoke with a lisp.) Years later, the squire claimed to have remained in the middle of the turmoil—hiding under a table. At another window, Otie Ford shouted, "I want my young 'un!" Pastor Anderson grabbed little Ruth and handed her out the window, saying, "Here, Otie; here, Otie!"

The fight ended as the men and boys, fearing sanctions, fled the scene. "I went out a window and saw Oscar Green bolt from another, and tear out of there in his T-Model," confessed Arnold. Frank and Claude Holt, along with John O'Neal, jumped in Claude's Chevy touring car and headed for Bradyville. "We stopped at the cave spring for water and several of the Bradyville boys were there washing up," said Arnold. One of them, apparently numb on home brew, kept asking, "Who'd I hit? Who'd I hit!?"

On Leather's initiative, most of the fighters were charged and eventually fined for being drunk and disorderly, destroying county property and reckless misconduct. At the hearing, the prosecutor interpreted fleeing the scene as an admission of guilt and asked one defendant, "Did you run?" The prompt answer was: "No, sir, I wasn't running, but I passed another fellow who sure was lightin' out of there!"

Frank Holt of Bradyville was characterized as "the cock of the walk" and a troublemaker. He said that he didn't understand what that meant but proudly admitted that he got in the "best licks." Luke Green, however, was probably the biggest winner. "I fi't all through it," he later boasted, "and got $2.36 for being a witness."

About the Author

Greg Tucker returned to his family's home county after retiring from an international litigation practice with the law firm of Covington & Burling in Washington, D.C. He now raises beef cattle and writes a weekly column about the people, places and events that make his home county unique. Greg and his wife, Minh-Triet, live in Donnells Chapel, a rural Rutherford County community.

Photography by Fletcher, Rowley & Chao.

Visit us at
www.historypress.net